{ THEY ARE US }

Lutherans and Immigration

Stephen Bouman and
Ralston Deffenbaugh

Foreword by Martin E. Marty

They Are Us

They Are Us

Lutherans and Immigration

Stephen Bouman

and

Ralston Deffenbaugh

AUGSBURG FORTRESS

MINNEAPOLIS

THEY ARE US
Lutherans and Immigration

Unless otherwise identified, scripture quotations are from the New Revised Standard Version Bible, copyright © 1989 by the division of Christian Education of the National Council of the Churches of Christ in the USA. Used by permission. All rights reserved.

Cover design: Brad Norr
Interior design: PerfecType, Nashville, TN

Library of Congress Cataloging-in-Publication Data

Bouman, Stephen Paul.
  They are us : Lutherans and immigration / Stephen Bouman and Ralston Deffenbaugh.
     p. cm.
  Includes bibliographical references.
  ISBN 978-0-8066-5763-9 (alk. paper)
  1. United States—Emigration and immigration—Religious aspects—Evangelical Lutheran Church in America. 2. Church work with immigrants—Evangelical Lutheran Church in America. 3. Emigration and immigration law—United States. 4. Church work with immigrants—United States. I. Deffenbaugh, Ralston H. II. Title.
  BX8074.B4B68 2009
  284.1'35086912—dc22
                                      2009006408

14   13   12   11   10   09   3   4   5   6

DEDICATION

To the immigrants and refugees among us
and to the great staff and partners of
Lutheran Immigration and Refugee Service
who daily carry out our Lord's call to "welcome the stranger."
They are us.
—Ralston Deffenbaugh

and

To my partners in
Evangelical Mission and Congregational Ministry unit of the ELCA
Missionary bishops and synod councils
Immigrant members of the congregations I have served
The Metropolitan New York Synod
My immigrant ancestors
—Stephen Paul Bouman

Contents

Acknowledgments

We all stand on the shoulders of those who have come before. With each of my now eighteen years of service at the helm of Lutheran Immigration and Refugee Service (LIRS), I am aware of that more and more. I give thanks to God for all that those before us have established and taught. It is indeed a blessing that the Lutheran church lifts up so high its ministries of justice and service for uprooted people.

Special words of thanks are due to the board and staff of LIRS for giving me the opportunity and time to coauthor this book. Among the staff I want to lift up LIRS executive vice president Annie Wilson, a great partner in leadership who took on additional administrative burdens while I was researching and writing; former LIRS special counsel for policy and advocacy Matt Wilch, who has played a major role in shaping LIRS's long-term advocacy goals and my own thinking on immigration issues; and LIRS executive assistant Connie Ward, who handles the scheduling and flow of work in my office and makes me more productive. LIRS policy and advocacy associate Katherine Ollenburger, a Mennonite Volunteer Service intern, did the interviewing and writing for the of vignettes about Lutheran congregations. LIRS director for church and community outreach Tara Mulder crafted the discussion questions found in the back of the book. Thanks to them all—they help make the great team that is LIRS.

Finally, my wife Miriam Boraas Deffenbaugh supports me and my work in ways impossible to enumerate. I could not do what I do without her. Thank you, Marby!

Ralston Deffenbaugh

I would like to thank the staff of the bishop's office of the Metropolitan New York Synod, the pastors and lay leaders of the immigration ministries of New York, and the members of its Immigration Task Force who served while I was bishop in New York. They made the issues real in the grassroots immigrant church.

For specific help in the writing of this book, I would also like to thank the following who shared their heart for mission in interviews: Pastors Ruben Duran, Gemeches Buba, Carlos Paiva, David Rommerein, Joe Garcia, and Bishop Steve Ullestad.

Stephen Bouman

Foreword

Writers of forewords are expected, even virtually commanded, to commend the book they are forwarding. If they are not ready to do so, they have no business accepting the assignment to write. So I will commend with enthusiasm *They Are Us.* Yet even the most enthusiastic commenders do not surrender their rights to be critical or to grumble a bit. I did not find much to criticize here and will get over my grumble—note the singular—right away. I confess to having had trouble with the title. Not with its idea, which is provocative, pointed, and pertinent, but with the grammar.

Thanks to a toy store and a character from the comics, we learned to say "Toys R Us," and from the late possum Pogo an observation has entered the vocabulary as a virtual mantra: "We have met the enemy and it is us." So embedded are such usages in our minds and habits that if we wanted to satisfy our elementary school grammar teachers and do it right, we would call this book *They Are We*—and risk sounding strange to the generations who grew up on the wrong usages.

There, that's out of the way. Now to the book.

Authors Bouman and Deffenbaugh are addressing a problem and asking a question posed by philosopher Alasdair MacIntyre: "I can only answer the question, 'What am I to do?'

if I can answer the prior question 'Of what story or stories do I find myself a part?' " Readers are all urged to see themselves as part of the story of immigration, particularly to the United States. Some may join the millions in America for whom any talk about immigrants is about others, aliens, strangers. We on the other hand are part of a story of homogeneous long-timers in America. It is *our* place for *our* story, and immigrants don't belong.

The authors salt these pages with excellent stories, some about their own encounters with immigrants. So I invite myself to do the same, by taking a census around the family table. If Harriet and I succeed in getting all thirty-two of "ours"— "blood"- children, adopted-fostered-step children and grand-children, great grandchildren and in-laws—we count seven among them as "immigrants," beneficiaries of legislated policy changes in the United States in 1965. We would sorely miss them from that table were immigrants excluded.

However, had I said "immigrants" without reference to the 1965 legislation, thirty-two of the thirty-two would have to be seen as immigrants. *Immigrants Are Us*, all of us.

And today, immigrants are seen as a problem, not always without reason. Everyone recognizes that not all doors of all nations can be wide open all the time and in all circumstances. But policy questions have to come in after, not before, we consider the meaning of immigration, the needs and rights of immigrants, and—though this is often forgotten—the gifts they bring to the republic.

The first word for Christians has to be Christian. The Lutheran accent in this publication invites a spin on the Chris-tian story. An important thing to say, but not the only thing to say, is that dealing with the immigrant on all levels, from the personal to the political, should somehow reflect the law of God and the gospel of Christ. Divine Law, first: any believers within the Old Testament tradition and responsive to the God of Israel learns from reading Scripture that anyone who was blocking the stranger or mistreating the alien—ancestors to today's immigrants—was committing one of the chief sins in the book: "Remember, Israel, you were once aliens." At the same time followers of the gospel of Jesus Christ *get* to welcome the stranger in his name, to practice hospitality, and to share in the gifts that come in the exchange with the stranger.

Saying that does not solve everything, and it would be foolish if the innocent-dove-Christians were not at least partly guileful-as-serpents, which politics calls us to be. "Guileful" is a rather heavily loaded term, a serpentine word that invites and inspires hissing sounds. Here it is used metaphorically for politics, since in the political order policies about immigrant issues are finally decided. Churches can propose policy and protest political profanations. They can turn their church buildings into sanctuaries, and their members should vote in office-holders and vote for policies congenial to Christian practices of hospitality. But in the end, the political order decides policy.

Saying so is not to demean politicians, advocates, and public figures who speak out and work on all sides of immigrant issues. Instead, we are making an effort to *locate* controversies, proposals, and dreams in the order of the *polis*, the human city. Politics does not save souls, does not forgive sins, does not make hearts glad. But those who are aware know that "politics" knows the dirty secret of history: violence. Politics is an effort through give-and-take, argument, winning-some-and-losing-some, and compromise to minimize the violence of history. We see plenty of that on the immigration front, where vigilantes kill by caprice, with zest, at will, and without authorization. We see it in the exploitation of would-be immigrants or those denied immigration, as they are exploited, sometimes packed like cattle in trucks or containers, beaten up by those who send them off or would keep them out. We know of it among "undocumented" aliens, who are at the mercies of the merciless.

So politics enters the scene, as the nation at its best struggles for the most just and fair and humane addresses to immigration issues and sets up welfare policies to help new immigrants find their way into the exchanges of life enjoyed by those who were immigrants some years before, or whose grandparents were—newcomers who have to establish themselves with help from others.

They Are Us sets out to achieve this, and I think it successfully does: it helps readers turn their customary thinking around. One could, as I did in the opening lines, start with the "Problem of the Immigrant" and then back up to see what Scriptures say about the stranger, the other, the alien, the refugee, the immigrant and his or her needs and rights. But this book starts with the "Presence of the Immigrant," or the one who would be immigrant, and tries to take the immigrants' humanity with utter seriousness—after which it is time to work out proposals and policies.

This book begins under Lutheran auspices, but the authors make clear that it invites company—immigrant work demands all the company it can get!—from other Christians. But I hope these others who are figuratively migrating onto Lutheran soil by reading stories with many Lutheran contexts will feel at home there and carry what they take from this book back to their own circles. Let me say that on this front, we Lutherans do not start from scratch. Garrison Keillor, the radio storyteller of *The Prairie Home Companion* has done us a service by re-teaching Lutherans not to brag. But he has also done us a disservice by portraying a Wobegon provincialism that shows citizens to be narrow-minded, spiritually cramped, and prejudiced.

That portrayal does not square with some of the facts. In the late 1970s I was on a presidential commission "on the 1980s," in the late years of the Carter administration. I was a cog in the wheel of the "Health, Education, and Welfare" subcommittee. When immigration "health, education, and welfare" issues came up and I was identified as a Lutheran, those in the know knew that Lutherans (thanks to the Lutheran Immigration and Refugee Service and the policies and generous hearts of thousands in thousands of congregations) had done much to attract, settle, and defend immigrants—even in or especially in the kinds of areas Keillor lovingly satirizes. I spend my years in the Midwest and Upper Midwest, where ethnic, cultural, and religious differences are vast, thanks to the welcome Lutherans and their Christian kin have helped extend.

I don't want to overplay this, or to pretend that all is well. I'm told that in a movie of 2009, a character grumbling about the presence and ways of Hmong immigrants is told that they were there thanks to the Lutherans. It was a one-liner, designed for a knowing laugh. It's nice to think enough has happened that Lutherans at their best get identified with immigrants, which they or their ancestors were. Now I hope this book will give more reason for such an identification to grow and become virtually proverbial, as the immigrant still waits at the door or in many cases suffers after having found a door legally opened. This book has a very personal address. After reading it, we might ask, "Who is the target, who are the prospects to be agents of hope?" The answer: *They Are We.*

Martin E. Marty

Introduction: What Rough Beast Slouching from Ground Zero?

Come to me, all you that are weary
and are carrying heavy burdens,
and I will give you rest.
Take my yoke upon you, and learn from me;
for I am gentle and humble in heart,
and you will find rest for your souls.
For my yoke is easy, and my burden is light.
—Matthew 11:28–30

Send these, the homeless, tempest-tossed to me,
I lift my lamp beside the golden door.
—Emma Lazarus (Inscribed on the Statue of Liberty)

A freezing rain whipped in on the wind from New York Harbor as we gathered at the Battery in lower Manhattan. Through bone chilling sleet we could see the lady in the harbor, an enduring iconic presence holding aloft the welcoming torch. It was the day after the President's State of the Union address in 2006, and New York's religious leaders and immigration advocates were holding a press conference to urge President Bush and Congress to enact humane immigration reform and to reject current legislation pending in Congress that would criminalize anyone offering help to undocumented neighbors.

Just a few blocks away, on a beautiful September day five years earlier, the Twin Towers had come tumbling down, destroying the lives of thousands. For a brief moment afterward, the world's attention and our own was focused on what mattered most: our shared humanity, our communal compassion, our deepest spiritual longings and hope. But too soon, all that changed. In the ripple effects of September 11, 2001, something ugly has emerged, slouching from Ground Zero: a hardening of the heart toward the immigrant stranger among us.

We became fearful, and in our fear we came to believe that our security can be achieved only through power, enforcement, a closing of the ranks, and a sealing of the borders. On this cold, rainy day, representatives from many religious traditions gathered to refute that belief and to give voice to a shared spiritual conviction that our mutual security is tied not to power and isolation but to the well-being and dignity of every child of God. We were gathered to ask our president, our leaders, and our fellow citizens: What kind of community is emerging from Ground Zero? What kind of communal future are we building together?

> Mere anarchy is loosed upon the world,
> The blood-dimmed tide is loosed, and everywhere
> The ceremony of innocence is drowned;
> The best lack all conviction, while the worst
> Are full of passionate intensity . . .
> And what rough beast, its hour come round at last
> Slouches toward Bethlehem to be born?"
> —William Butler Yeats, *The Second Coming*[1]

What kind of a world is coming to birth in the changed communal landscape following September 11? A world where the rough beast of fearful exclusion slouches across the landscape both here and abroad? If so, that world must be resisted.

This book calls for a better world. It advocates a future in which how we welcome the stranger among us will be the primary issue determining how America emerges from the ashes of Ground Zero. How we welcome and regard the stranger among us is of primary importance for the church as well and one for which we believe our beloved Lutheran tradition has a ready answer. We are Lutheran and we are pro-immigrant.

Although our religious tradition is Lutheran, the invitation and reach of this book is broad and inclusive. It includes all who are in touch with their own immigrant forebears and who share deeply spiritual hopes for our communal life together.

Our Lutheran ancestors emigrated largely from northern Europe, many landing first in Bay Ridge, Brooklyn, across the bay from the Battery in Lower Manhattan. This country welcomed them. Because of that welcome, today congregations in the ELCA Metropolitan New York Synod worship in twenty-five languages. The Nordic and Germanic languages of our early immigrant forebears have given way to other tongues—Spanish, Arabic, Swahili, Mandarin, Korean, and others. But regardless of the language spoken, the message is the same: "Thank you. Thank you for welcoming us. Thank you for a new beginning."

Kamy Moghbelli, an Iranian immigrant, expressed his thanks in a hearing sponsored by the Immigration Task Force of the Metropolitan New York Synod:

> Good evening. This is my life. Yesterday: war, oppression, terror, escape, starvation. Today: food, shelter, protection, hope. Tomorrow: new beginning. I share a piece of my

mind from the heart of an immigrant and refugee. My name is Kamy Moghbelli. I am a refugee from Iran who came to the United States of America on February 24, 1984, with my wife and my son and daughter, the ages of three and one. We came to this country with little cash and seven suitcases after living in West Germany for four years and being shifted from one refugee camp to another. We were living there with Polish friends at the time of Solidarity, with friends from Afghanistan after the Russian invasion, with friends who were Kurds from Iraq, with friends from Iran. Now I am standing in front of you to say that I am proud to be a citizen of the greatest country in the world, the United States of America. I am also proud that I became a Christian and a Lutheran in this country. Because of my faith, I believe that God's grace, love, and care have been given to all God's children through Jesus Christ.[2]

After Kamy shared the story of his family's personal struggles, including near starvation, he ended his testimony with an unvarnished appeal to human solidarity: "Love starts at our tables, at our homes, at our meals that we share together." Indeed, they are us.

We believe that we are having the wrong conversation in our country about immigration today. It is a conversation driven by fear and often manipulated cynically by our political leaders. Yes, security is important, but at what price? How much are we willing to pay for the illusion that we can be totally secure? How many walls can we build? Where is the moral, political, and religious leadership? It is far too easy to bypass legitimate concerns about the world and to play the role of policy wonks, divided by this or that agenda.

The church too often is silent as politicians build public constituencies on a communal fear of the stranger. Our church bodies pass public statements on immigration while we ignore opportunities for real grassroots conversation among us. We talk about "them" as if they were faceless, voiceless beings, forgetting—perhaps by choice—that they too are children of God. We cannot—or will not—see Kamy's face and hear his voice. The global debate over immigration, economic migration, and a new emerging America is begging for Christian insight, faith, and courage. This book moves us into that more ambitious conversation.

Before we take on a broken immigration system, we must hear the clear call of God to practice radical hospitality. Scripture is not ambiguous about this issue. We may be divided on how to sort out today's immigration mess, but when the stranger knocks at the door, Christians instinctively open the door and attend to the immediate needs of the other. In this book you will meet churches and ministries that open the door. We will once more be refreshed by a biblical view of Jesus' community, where the only requirement for entrance is being human. As Martin Luther noted, when hospitality is given to the persecuted and oppressed, "God Himself is in our home, is being fed at our house, is lying down and resting."[3]

We also will lift up holy memories of our ancestors and their journey to this country, seeking connections between the dreams of our grandparents and the dreams of our new neighbors today. Memory and the hope it engenders can heal us. Like Rachel, who gleefully announced "I found us!" after discovering her family name among the endless list of immigrant names on the wall at Ellis Island, we find ourselves again as a nation and a church of immigrants when we welcome the stranger.

Welcoming the stranger can revive tired denominations. The strangers, our new neighbors, bring immense spiritual gifts with them. Max Weber's thesis of *disenchantment*—that modern society will no longer need the palliative of religion in this new secular age—is turned on its head. Many of our new neighbors bring vibrant faith, love of Scripture, and deeply evangelical hearts. Immigration means spiritual *re-enchantment*.

We encounter in our new neighbors a faith that blossoms in the midst of struggle and sometimes great danger and suffering. Migrants die in the Sonoran desert. Desperate people from Chiapas, Central America, whose families have little to eat and even less hope, gather in church basements in Agua Prieta, Mexico, on the night before their attempt to cross the border. Those who survive the desperate journey mow our lawns, do construction work on our houses, wash our dishes, and harvest our food. Many of our new neighbors—often living lives of silent despair as we turn our backs on them and blame them—lean on deep spiritual traditions and call on the name of the Lord as we do.

Once we have encountered our biblical roots as followers of Jesus, and our primal ancestral roots in solidarity with our new neighbors, we will take up our broken immigration system. We need a better public conversation, a conversation that makes migration a positive experience both for migrants and for the nations that send and receive them. Migration should be safe, positive, legal, regulated, humane, and hopefully one day unnecessary. This conversation must bring together political parties, businesses, labor, immigrant communities, and the spiritual imagination of our many religious traditions.

On that chilly day at the Battery, with the Statue of Liberty as a backdrop, a vision was shared for the kind of community we seek. A community where all people, united in faith and in the memory of our immigrant grandparents, work together for the good of all Americans. A vision sharing these modest hopes:

- An opportunity for our hardworking neighbors—who already contribute to this country—to emerge from the shadows and to pursue an legal residence and even citizenship.
- Reforms that keep families together rather than breaking them apart.
- Legal ways for people who want to work and need to feed their families to enter our country in an orderly way with their rights protected.
- Border policies that are not an extension of vigilante fear; policies that keep out those who would harm us while treating all with respect and dignity.

As Stephen said on that cold, wet, windy day in Battery Park in 2006:

> In particular, today I want our senators to know that they have allies here—red and blue state people whose faith unites them and whose grateful memories of their grandparents make them ready to be partners in a new vision for all of us to emerge from Ground Zero.[4]

What manner of community will emerge from a landscape that changed dramatically after September 11, 2001? We envision a community that offers a haven for every refugee, a job for every migrant, a home for every immigrant, a vision that is profoundly biblical and deeply faithful.

We want to thank you for your openness to this critical conversation on immigration. We approach this conversation from many different viewpoints, which is to be expected in the great diversity and universal reach of Christ's body. As we learn to welcome the stranger among us, we will be transformed into deeper community at the foot of the cross.

{ 1 }

Walking in Newness of Life

Walking amid the scream of engines and machines at Ground Zero, you look up and are shocked by the immensity of the destruction and carnage. The rubble slows you down, but you keep walking, wanting to help, wanting to comfort. There is no consolation, no happy ending to tack on, nothing uplifting to grasp. But there is this: moving feet bring resurrection hope. And there is this: we have already been buried alive, baptized into the death of Christ, in order that we might get back on our feet and move into God's future.

> Do you not know that all of us who have been baptized into Christ Jesus were baptized into his death? Therefore we have been buried with him by baptism into death, so that, just as Christ was raised from the dead by the glory of the Father, *we too might walk in newness of life.* For if we have been united with him in a death like his, we will certainly be united with him in a resurrection like his. (Romans 6:3-5, emphasis added)

At Ground Zero, people from every corner of the earth were united in death, in loss and burial—the ultimate solidarity. In spite of this profound solidarity, however, slouching from Ground Zero came the rough beast of fear and rejection of the stranger, a fracturing of human solidarity. But the many feet walking together through loss and grief still bring resurrection hope. This book is written in resurrection hope. We write with confidence and faith in the gospel of God's promises. It is from that perspective that we want to engage you in ways that invite you and your church to join both the conversation about immigration and the ministry to immigrants—with your hearts and minds but also with your feet.

The Exodus Event and the Christ Event

We look first through two biblical lenses that focus our vision on the call of God to welcome the stranger, to serve the oppressed, to accompany the unfortunate in our midst. For Christians, the call to respond positively to the needs of both documented and undocumented immigrants, refugees, and those fleeing persecution and seeking asylum is not ideologically based—it is biblically mandated.

"You Shall Also Love the Stranger"

The foundational event for the Hebrew people is the Exodus out of slavery in Egypt into the freedom of the Promised Land—an event driven by the compassion of God:

> Then the LORD said, "I have observed the misery of my people who are in Egypt; I have heard their cry on account of their taskmasters. Indeed, I know their sufferings, and I have come down to deliver them from

the Egyptians, and to bring them up out of that land to
a good and broad land, a land flowing with milk and
honey. (Exodus 3:7-8)

Here is the dream of the downtrodden, the oppressed, the
exploited, the enslaved, the poor: "a land flowing with milk
and honey," a land where freedom, opportunity, human dignity, fullness of life, and wellbeing are not just ideas but are
realities grounded in just laws.

The Exodus from slavery to freedom became the linchpin
of Hebrew identity. From generation to generation—even to
the present day—the memory of the Exodus is kept alive in
both the Jewish and Christian traditions not as ancient history
but as *our history,* as *our story*:

> When your children ask you in time to come, "What is
> the meaning of the decrees and the statutes and the ordi-
> nances that the LORD our God has commanded you?" then
> you shall say to your children, "We were Pharaoh's slaves
> in Egypt, but the LORD brought us out of Egypt with a
> mighty hand.... He brought us out from there in order
> to bring us in, to give us the land that he promised on
> oath to our ancestors. Then the LORD commanded us to
> observe all these statutes, to fear the LORD our God, for
> our lasting good, so as to keep us alive, as is now the
> case. If we diligently observe this entire commandment
> before the LORD our God, as he has commanded us, we
> will be in the right. (Deuteronomy 6:20-21, 23-25)

The "decrees and the statutes and the ordinances" given to
the newly freed Hebrews by their just, liberating, and saving
God were many. For our purposes here, we note that the laws
of Israel's God show a "preferential option" for the stranger,
the alien, the poor, and defenseless. Several texts can be mar-
shaled to make the point quickly:

For the LORD your God is God of gods and Lord of lords, the great God, mighty and awesome, who is not partial and takes no bribe, who executes justice for the orphan and the widow, and *who loves the strangers*, providing them food and clothing. *You shall also love the stranger, for you were strangers in the land of Egypt.* (Deuteronomy 10:17-19, emphasis added)

You shall not wrong or oppress a resident alien, for you were aliens in the land of Egypt. You shall not abuse any widow or orphan. (Exodus 22:21-22, emphasis added)

When an alien resides with you in your land, you shall not oppress the alien. *The alien who resides with you shall be to you as the citizen among you; you shall love the alien as yourself,* for you were aliens in the land of Egypt: I am the LORD your God. (Leviticus 19:33-34, emphasis added)

We could go on listing texts, but the point is clear. Caring for the alien, the stranger, the oppressed is not an option for people of Jewish or Christian faith—it is God's will. The plight of the dispossessed matters to God. It must matter to God's people.

Our love of the stranger is grounded both in God's love for us and in *our own personal or ancestral experience of being strangers in a strange land.* This is generally true of all who call themselves either Jew or Christian; it is particularly true of those who also call themselves American. We are a nation of immigrants. Our roots are in other places and our ancestors' stories of migration are our stories. Above all others, Americans should be predisposed to feel the struggle, the fear, the suffering, and the hopes and dreams of all those who, in one way or another, make it to this country.

As we address the plight of today's documented and undocumented immigrant populations, we stand in line with those of
whom the ancient Hebrew poet wrote:

> Happy are those whose help is the God of Jacob,
>   whose hope is in the LORD their God...
>   who executes justice for the oppressed;
>   who gives food to the hungry.
> The LORD sets the prisoners free;
>   the LORD opens the eyes of the blind.
> The LORD lifts up those who are bowed down;
>   the LORD loves the righteous.
> The LORD *watches over the strangers*;
>   he upholds the orphan and the widow. . .
> (Psalm 146:5, 7-9, emphasis added)

As we welcome and care for the strangers among us, God is
our help, our hope, and our example.

"And the Word Became Flesh and Lived among Us"

The foundational event in the history of Christian people is the
Christ event: the incarnation, life, teaching, suffering, death,
and resurrection of Jesus of Nazareth. Through the lens of the
Christ event, we see God and know who we are and what we
are called to do.

Remember that Jesus was a Jew, and he shared the passion
for justice and concern for the stranger found in the Hebrew
Bible (our Old Testament) that we highlighted above. Jesus
inaugurated his public ministry by quoting from the Hebrew
prophet Isaiah:

> When he came to Nazareth, where he had been brought
> up, he went to the synagogue on the Sabbath day, as was

his custom. He stood up to read, and the scroll of the prophet Isaiah was given to him. He unrolled the scroll and found the place where it was written:

"The Spirit of the Lord is upon me,
        because he has anointed me
        to bring good news to the poor.
He has sent me to proclaim release to the captives
        and recovery of sight to the blind,
        to let the oppressed go free,
        to proclaim the year of the Lord's favor."

And he rolled up the scroll, gave it back to the attendant, and sat down. The eyes of all in the synagogue were fixed on him. Then he began to say to them, "Today this scripture has been fulfilled in your hearing." (Luke 4:16-21)

Jesus' story, as recorded in the four Gospels, is the story of welcome, of inclusion, of hospitality, of service to both Jew and Gentile, to citizens of Israel and to the strangers in their midst, particularly those who were considered outsiders, unclean and not worthy of human dignity. According to biblical scholar John Dominic Crossan, a chief characteristic of Jesus' way with the world was "open commensality," that is, an open table, "an eating together without using table as a miniature map of society's vertical discriminations and lateral separations."[1]

As you will discover, the metaphor of the table as a place of welcome and hospitality, as a place of meeting between strangers, is a key theme of this book. The metaphor comes from the ministry of Jesus. "No one was excluded from Jesus' table except those who excluded themselves. The only ones who didn't experience the good food, good wine, and good times at Jesus' table were those who thought they were too good to eat and drink (let alone talk to) the folks who joyfully sat down to table with him."[2] Jesus' table is our table; our table is Jesus' table where all are welcome.

When pressed to say which was the greatest commandment, Jesus replied: " 'You shall love the Lord your God with all your heart, and with all your soul, and with all your mind.' This is the greatest and first commandment. And a second is like it: 'You shall love your neighbor as yourself.' On these two commandments hang all the law and the prophets" (Matthew 22:37-40). Jesus was quoting from the Hebrew scriptures (Deuteronomy 6:5 and Leviticus 19:18), making it crystal clear that love is the cornerstone of religious life. In the second greatest commandment, "You shall love your neighbor as yourself," we find a concrete application of this law: "You shall love the alien as yourself" (Leviticus 19:34). This is not an option for people of faith. It is God's will.

Jesus told his followers that when they fed the hungry, gave drink to the thirsty, welcomed the stranger, clothed the naked, and visited the sick and those in prison, they were doing it to him. When they failed to do these things, they failed to serve him (Matthew 25:31-45). What better text to ground a theology of solidarity with documented and undocumented immigrants? In Micah 6:8 we are told that God requires of us only three things:

> He has told you, O mortal, what is good;
> and what does the LORD require of you
> but to do justice, and to love kindness,
> and to walk humbly with your God?

Jesus' life interprets this text. This text should shape our lives. When it does, we meet the strangers among us with humility, love, and justice.

Friends on Foot

Many modern lives mirror God's love for the stranger and ground immigration ministry in the great narratives of Scripture and in the narratives of our own ancestors. One such ministry is "Amigos En Pie," which means "friends on foot," or "friends on the road." Amigos En Pie is sponsored by Trinity Lutheran Church on 100th Street in Manhattan. Their pastor, Heidi Neumark, is a long distance runner in immigration ministry.

The parish's ministry of welcome is centered in Spanish-language Sunday worship. Entrance to the offices of Amigos En Pie are right off the sanctuary; the altar and font are literally linked to this ministry. During the week, legal assistance, children's programs, English and literacy programs, and many other programs that keep soul and body together are offered to immigrants by immigrant leaders.

Many of our new neighbors have been on their feet for a long time and they need "friends on the road," amigos en pie. Perhaps they started on the road as economic migrants in El Salvador or Costa Rica or Mexico. Perhaps they got up one morning in Agua Prieto, Mexico, on the Arizona border, and their feet took them through the Sonoran desert, an act of courage we can hardly comprehend.

Many of our new neighbors have walked from teeming refugee camps. Many have run from persecution and political oppression. Many have traveled on foot through this country, a country that barely notices them. Many weary feet have trudged to incarceration after midnight immigration raids. Many discover that they have come to a country that is afraid, turns its back on them, and blames them for coming here. We call those without documents "illegal." We even use the word "terrorist" and "immigrant" in the same sentence, in the same law.

The church must meet all God's children in solidarity. Our grandparents, great-grandparents, and our new immigrant neighbors have walked the same path that many in the Bible walked.

- Abraham and Sarah were economic migrants, leaving the land of their family because God had promised them a new and prosperous land. In a time of severe famine, they "went down to Egypt to reside there as an alien" (Genesis 12:10).
- Joseph's brothers also got on their feet in a land where people were starving to death. They too were economic migrants who went to Egypt.
- Moses, escaping possible imprisonment or capital death in Egypt, fled to the land of Midian, where he met and married a woman of that land. She bore a son, and Moses named him Gershom, a Hebrew name that means "alien," for he said, "I have been an alien residing in a foreign land" (Exodus 2:22).
- The Israelites were driven into exile in Babylon where they lamented: "How could we sing the LORD's song in a foreign land?" (Psalm 137:4).
- Mary and Joseph, the parents of Jesus, took their baby and fled from political oppression.
- Paul and the other apostles traveled throughout the Mediterranean region in service of Christ's gospel. As strangers on the road, they were dependent on the mercy of local residents and in constant danger from those who were fearful and suspicious of them.

The Bible is full of companions on the road. We must link the feet of our biblical ancestors with the feet of our immigrant grandparents and with the feet of our new neighbors.

Telling Ancestor Stories

Our immigrant roots go way back: "A wandering Aramean was my ancestor; he went down into Egypt and lived there as an alien, few in number" (Deuteronomy 26:5). His name was Abraham; if you call yourself Jew or Christian or Muslim, he is your ancestor. His story is your story.

Abraham and Sarah led their family toward a land of promise, toward a new life, survival, and redemption. This trek is repeated in the heat of the Sonoran desert, in boats from Africa running ashore in southern Europe, in boats sailing from Cuba to Florida, in river crossings, in ships from Fujian province heading to Los Angeles or Manhattan. Along the trek, in strange places with strange names like Schechem and Bethel, Abraham and Sarah found hope, welcome, and signs of God's grace and presence. At each place of hope and refreshment they built an altar and called on the name of God.

Schechem and Bethel today are in the undercroft at Gloria Dei Lutheran Church in Huntington Station, Long Island, where homeless refugees are given shelter, comfort, and dignity. They are in Brewster, New York, where faithful people organize to fight their own municipality for the privilege of taking in and welcoming the stranger with bed and meal. Schechem and Bethel, places of God's grace and presence, can be found in Amigos En Pie, the immigrant ministry of Trinity Lutheran, 100th Street; they can be found in Amagansett, on the east end of Long Island, where people of faith listen to the stories of economic migrants rousted out of their homes in the middle of the night. Schechem and Bethel are in congregations in Brooklyn and Los Angeles involved in the sanctuary movement, offering hospitality and safety to vulnerable families; they are in Fargo and Denver, where congregations welcome the "lost boys" of

Sudan. Bethel. Schechem. A trail of altars marking hope and the presence of God. A wandering Aramean, his wife and family are our ancestors in the faith. We find ourselves as we read of Abraham and Sarah's migration, the beginning of our family of faith's journey. The altars at which we worship on the Lord's Day are our Schechem and Bethel, places of refreshment and hope, signs of divine grace and presence.

Jews and Christians remember who we are and what God does for us by remembering, by never forgetting that we were slaves, exiles, economic migrants. Telling the ancestors' stories not only keeps the memory alive but tells us who we are, where we come from, and where God is leading us. Telling the ancestors' story continues in the New Testament (read Acts 7).

In this context, we learn how to treat the alien today. Don't forget your ancestors! Don't forget God's covenant faithfulness to them when they were aliens in a strange land. Remember that their story is your story. Remember that it was the church that welcomed them and helped them make a new beginning in a new land.

Scripture also invites us to think about the table as we tell ancestor stories. In the Jewish tradition, the Seder or Passover meal hinges on this question, asked by a child: "Why is this night unlike every other night?" The child then answers with the story of the Passover, which is told as if every person around the table was there when it happened: "On this night God saved me. . ."

Think of the kitchen table in your own home. In our home it is where we developed our identity. Over the table, over the years, we heard ancestor stories, we sang songs, we discussed the day, we made plans. At the table our values were formed, hard questions were asked and answered. At the table we became a family. The altar table in your congregation unites all the kitchen tables of the parish and of the world. At this table we hear ancestor stories, sing songs, share family meals, form identities as disciples of Jesus. Grace, forgiveness, generosity, and abundance emanate from this altar table. Immigrants and non-immigrants, we receive here Christ's unconditional promises.

The Kingdom on the Left, the Kingdom on the Right

Immigration issues are complex. It is helpful to remember that Lutherans have two ways of looking at them. In the kingdom on the left (the realm of civil law), we struggle with others of good will to craft proposals for comprehensive immigration reform that are fair and just and protect human rights. In the kingdom on the left, there is much for people of good will to discuss and argue about as we seek to create effective and humane policies. We do this work with humility, knowing that we could be wrong about this or that approach, knowing that what we actually can achieve may fall short of the best possible outcome. From the kingdom on the left, we propose a few guiding principles for comprehensive immigration reform:

- We recognize the need for homeland security but not at the expense of people's rights; harsh and punitive treatment is beneath the dignity of a nation of immigrants.
- We believe in family values and want immigration reform that protects families and keeps them together, reuniting them when they have been separated.
- We want to end the marginalization of the undocumented who huddle in the shadows, barely surviving in fear.
- We want a path toward permanence, a mechanism allowing those who contribute to our country's economy and society to live full and open lives.

We can agree on these principles and then disagree on this or that policy to implement them. In the kingdom on the right (the realm of the gospel), however, people who might disagree on policy together hear the God of the Bible call us to welcome the stranger. Compassion, solidarity, and generosity of spirit should come naturally to grandchildren of a wandering Aramean. You cannot love God while rejecting those God embraces:

> Those who say, "I love God," and hate their brothers or sisters, are liars; for those who do not love a brother or sister whom they have seen, cannot love God whom they have not seen. The commandment we have from him is this: those who love God must love their brothers and sisters also. (1 John 4:20-21)

Strangers in a Strange Land

To be a stranger in a strange land is to be on the gangplank between worlds, to be at the threshold between what lies behind and what lies ahead. To be a stranger in a strange land is to live between memory and hope.

- It is a time of choice and vulnerability.
- It is a time of looking backward and either demonizing or idealizing the past, the home country.
- It is a time of looking forward with a mix of fear and excitement, a mix of dreams and dread.
- It is a time to watch your step, to be careful, to be busy learning the cultural cues and rules of living in a new place.
- It is a time to dream of new beginnings in a new land.

The mission of the church is found at this threshold.

Finding New Roots

All immigrants are uprooted (often violently) and planted in a new place. The uprooting is disorienting. One of our founding fathers is alleged to have said: "You declared independence when you got on the boat." It is indeed a dizzying leap of faith. The uprooting might be long and violent, but new roots in the soil of America can grow deeply. The church must be a place to water and nourish those new roots.

Bringing the Ordeal of Passage to an End

It has been said that it took forty days for the Israelites to get out of slavery, but it took forty years to get slavery out of the Israelites. It was a long and difficult ordeal of passage, geographically and spiritually. It still is. Daily people risk their lives to cross borders and too often die on the journey. Mostly they are desperately poor, trying to save the lives of their children or feed their parents. They are the biblical Ruth and her mother-in-law seeking food in the land of Moab; Joseph's brothers crossing the border into Egypt in search of survival in a time of famine. It takes great courage and faith to step inside a church where others worship, especially in a foreign language. If they are welcomed, it is a sign that the ordeal of passage is ending. If they are excluded, it is a sign that the ordeal continues.

Ending Bad Situations

At a memorial service in Queens, New York, people from the Congo mourned the loss of hundreds of thousands, including family members—all the victims of insane violence in East Africa. Many of our grandfathers and great-grandfathers remember leaving Europe to avoid military conscription as cannon fodder for European wars they did not believe in. Many of our grandparents got on a ship, left difficult lives behind, and sought a better future for themselves and their families—just like today's immigrants, refugees, and asylum seekers.

Being Welcomed

The church can help people cross cultural divides and learn from difference, a place where we experience that "different" does not mean "right" or "wrong," it just means different. The church's welcome of the stranger should always be expectant, trusting that the strangers come bearing gifts wrapped in the colors and customs of another place. The one who is welcomed becomes the welcomer.

Being Safe

Many people come to this country with battered and scarred bodies, the victims of war, thuggish governments, ethnic and religious violence, and the ordeal of passage. They come fleeing gang wars in El Salvador and Honduras, crime waves in Lagos, genocide in too many places. All too often, bodily harm does not stop at the U.S. border. In Farmingville, Long Island, local men have lured Mexicans to phony jobs and beat them to death. Young Fujianese teens tell of fellow migrants who have committed suicide.

There is security in having a purse or wallet stuffed with credit cards. There is safety in having an officially sanctioned identity card. Many immigrants have no such tokens of security. Our churches must take an objective census of the bodies living in their vicinity. Our neighbors' safety is our concern.

Building Connected Lives

Many immigrants build new relationships through the church, through a network of connections with other Christians. Religion means literally to "tie fast," to "connect." The church connects people to each other and to God, ties them fast to the community of God's people. Travelers might arrive alone, but they must soon be brought into the body of Christ. The church is Bethel and Schechem, a place of welcome, hope, and divine presence where our grandparents began to live connected lives and where today's immigrants must also find a home.

Finding a Path through the Maze

With the help of the church our grandparents made a stand, found their first apartments and jobs, cut through red tape, and learned to live in American society. Every congregation can be a place that helps new neighbors cut a path through the impossible thickets of life. Finding and working with immigration lawyers, learning English, finding a case manager, discovering advocates for immigrant housing or health care is a daunting task for those new to this country. Early childhood programs, summer Bible schools, Sunday Schools, confirmation classes, and youth groups can be places where immigrant parents find allies in raising children in a new land.

Honoring the Dignity of All

We were all created in the image of God and all deserve the dignity that comes with being a beloved child of God. But the stranger is often anonymous; unnoticed, discounted, or treated as beneath contempt. How should the church regard over twelve million economic migrants who are without documents?

If they are regarded as criminals, it is all too easy to dehumanize and demonize them. If they are regarded as beloved children of God, we will accept them as members of our own family: "you shall love the alien as yourself" (Leviticus 19:34). "Be Not Afraid" is a congregation based program, jointly sponsored by Lutheran Immigration and Refugee Service and the ELCA, to help immigrants whose lives and often families have been torn apart by immigration raids. It is a harsh reality that cries out for the compassionate presence and action of the church.

Walking in Newness of Life

Immigrants of every generation, all the way back to Abraham and Sarah and their family, have experienced similar physical, psychological, and spiritual struggles. The church that assists the migrant, the refugee, the asylum-seeker has the resurrection power to turn their arduous trek into a pilgrimage of hope. The church that turns its face to the stranger is a church renewed and reformed. This book calls the church to embrace our new neighbors and to *walk with them* in newness of life. Walking in newness of life is not only a metaphor—it means walking into God's future in solidarity with those whom society considers to be "the least of these."

{ 2 }

A Church of Immigrants[1]

For many Lutherans in the United States, the memory of immigration is still alive in themselves, their families, and their congregations. Parents or grandparents may still speak the language of their homeland while the children speak English. There may still be contacts with relatives in foreign countries. Special foods are still eaten on special occasions. Older church buildings may still have stained glass inscriptions in German or Scandinavian model ships hanging from the ceiling. Because of our immigrant heritage and our embrace of the profound biblical and theological grounds for "welcoming the stranger," the Lutheran church has a special involvement with immigration and refugee matters.

This involvement is as old as Biblical times—the people of Israel were refugees from Egypt, the Holy Family refugees to Egypt. It was reinforced in Reformation times—Luther himself had to be spirited away and given sanctuary at the Wartburg Castle. It was demonstrated in suffering and service at the end of World War II, when one out of every six Lutherans in the world was a refugee. It continues to this day through the work of the Lutheran World Federation (LWF), Lutheran Immigration and Refugee Service (LIRS), and the many Lutheran congregations and individuals who reach out a hand of welcome to the newcomers around them.

Why People Emigrate: Family, Work, and Freedom

So why do people make the wrenching decision to leave their homelands and come to the United States? We can imagine at least three reasons—for family, for work, and for freedom. Overlaid on these are "push" and "pull" factors—the extent to which people are pushed to leave their country and pulled to America.

Family

Family ties are a powerful impetus for emigration. Family members leave home to be reunited with family who emigrated earlier. People from different places fall in love and want to be together. Family emigrate to become caretakers for an elderly or ill relative who can no longer live independently.

Work

As people pursue their livelihoods and make their way in the world, sometimes they see an opportunity in another country for a better living, or for more interesting work, or simply for adventure. Oftentimes, the work in a foreign country may be temporary, with the worker having no intention of immigrating permanently. But sometimes people put down roots in a new country and the migration becomes permanent. Push and pull factors can be at play here, especially when people are trying to escape poverty and to provide for themselves and their families in a new land.

Freedom

Migration is not always voluntary. Throughout human history, even today sadly, people have been forced to leave their homes. They flee political or religious persecution, hunger, or natural disaster. Having been pushed out of their native lands, they hope to return soon. But all too often that is not possible. The Statue of Liberty in New York Harbor is an extraordinarily powerful symbol of America's welcome for those who come here wanting to breathe free.

Two Stories from the Narrative of Immigration

It is fascinating to read the journals of immigrants. The details of particular stories are as varied as the people who left one home for another. But the broad themes of the narrative of immigration are repeated again and again, as illustrated by our own family stories.

Ralie's Story

Ralie is the great-grandson of immigrants who in the 1870s moved from Bohemia to New York City, where they met and married in 1881. Soon after, they traveled west to New Prague, Minnesota, where Ralie's grandfather, Fred Funda, was born. Ralie's great-grandfather migrated for a combination of the three reasons discussed above:

- He migrated for freedom. Bohemia was then a part of the Austro-Hungarian Empire, and the emperor was seeking to induct strong young men into his army. Ralie's great-grandfather, a good Czech patriot, was not excited about fighting foreign wars for a foreign emperor.

- He migrated for family. Some relatives had already migrated to America and said he could join them.
- He migrated for work. His relatives spoke of ample opportunity for an industrious young man willing to apply himself.

Young Fred Funda was born in the United States but spoke Czech as his first language. He did not learn English until he entered public elementary school. His father died young. His mother and her two young children were taken in by relatives, first in North Dakota and then in Oklahoma. Fred continued to speak Czech with his mother until she died, but otherwise his adult life was conducted in English. He graduated from what is now Oklahoma State University, became a civil engineer, served in the U.S. Army in France in World War I, helped build the Cuba Railroad (a migrant worker, albeit as an engineer!), and spent most of his career back in the United States with the Rock Island Line. He married an American whose ancestors came from England before the Revolution. He did not try to teach Czech to his daughter, Ralie's mother.

This pattern of integration remains typical for immigrants today. Those who migrate speak their native language at home. Their children speak the native language with their parents and English at school and with friends. The public schools are a major vehicle for Americanization. When it is time to marry, the children of immigrants often fall in love outside their immigrant group. The immigrants' grandchildren usually speak only English.

Stephen's Story

Stephen's paternal grandparents, Magdalena Erdmann and Henry Janssen Bouman, met in America. Magdalena was born in Theresa, Wisconsin. Her father was a farmer from West Prussia, her mother a farmer's daughter from Pomerania. Both were born in 1836. They met and married in their new country, after emigrating here in the 1850s.

Stephen's grandfather, Heinrich, was born in Norden, Germany, and came to America with his parents, Johann Hinrich Bouman and Anna Rebekka Schomann. They settled in Clara City, Minnesota, among a colony of East Friesian immigrants. Johann had inherited a farm in Norden, right up against the North Sea Dikes. He was not a very good farmer, the dike taxes were onerous, and Prussia was always recruiting young men for their growing military ambitions. These were the years of German imperialism under Bismarck and Kaiser Friedrich Wilhelm II. Taxes and conscription rates were both rising. For these and other reasons, Johann and "Anchen" believed that they could provide a better life for their children by emigrating to America.

Networks from the homeland and church networks were important in helping my forebears in America get started, acquire land, and make a life in the new country. But life was still hard. In 1951 Bernhard Martin Bouman, an engineer and younger brother of Heinrich, wrote a journal about his life in Norden, Germany, and about their emigration when he was thirteen to Clara City, Minnesota. A few excerpts give the flavor of life in transition.

> It was in March, in the year 1890, when father and mother told us that it had been decided to go to America—to Minnesota. I was then thirteen years old. At first I was glad to hear this for I had read a great many Indian stories and

stories of the great prairies of the west. Here was adventure. But then came thoughts of father and mother—what it must mean to them. It had been increasingly difficult to obtain the funds necessary to meet all the payments when due, so they decided to sell when they could see no way out. . . .

Then the day of the auction was there. Mother's ancestral porcelain and the century old rosewood cabinets, the old oak cabinets and all the things that had come down from families of the past were sold. . . . It was then that the full pain of leaving the old place and the old country came over me. But what is painful is often the beginning of the greatest blessing. We were becoming citizens of the United States of America!

In the early morning, a few days after the auction, a number of neighbors came to take the family and its boxes to the station on the way to Bremen. . . . [T]he sea was very rough and I became seasick just as soon as I caught a whiff of the smell on the big ship and I remained sick for ten days until we approached land. . . .

Of New York, where we stayed three days, I remember only the harbor and the elevated trains pulled by puffing steam engines. I also remember my great appetite after my ten day fast at sea. The train from New York to Clara City, Minnesota took four days. The train left us off at the tiny "depot" at midnight. Besides the "depot," there were two stores, a few houses, and a small church. It was the pastor of this church who had corresponded with father about a farm there. One of the stores functioned as a hotel, whose proprietor was a Hollander so we could understand each other. He put up a wonderful table and only charged us fifty cents per person. Here father bought farm equipment, groceries, flour and all that was necessary. The next day being Sunday, we went to church. After the church services were over, the minister spoke to some of the farmers after he had introduced us. So they came the next day to transport our belongings to a farm six miles away. . . .

There was not much room in our new house, which had a kitchen, living room, and a small bedroom downstairs. Upstairs, under the rafters, there was just a general attic which we curtained off into two parts to separate the sheep from the goats. There were nine of us. . . .

In July of our first year on the farm, we received visits from Indians. They were members of a party of men, women, and children who were camping at Willow Lake, about two miles south of us. At first, three men came to the farm and asked for hay. Father gave them all they could carry. The next day, a number of women came asking for flour, sugar and salt. Mother gave them as much as she could spare. On the third day, the women came again, bringing their babies all dressed up and washed clean. This time, they brought presents that they had made themselves, such as knives, made of a soft reddish stone. It was evident that they wished to show their friendliness. Of course, it was necessary to use the sign language. . . .

One of those children in the drafty loft in their new home in America, Heinrich Janssen, Stephen's grandfather, went to school and became a pastor. He met his wife, Magdalena in Verden, South Dakota, where he was a vicar. They married and lived in parsonages in Sabeca, Minnesota; Freeman, South Dakota; and Hamburg, Minnesota, where Stephen's father was born. Stephen's father became a Lutheran school teacher and church musician and met his wife at his first position in Milwaukee. Her father's family came from Hermansburg, Germany, and her mother's father, Friedrich Pfotenhauer, came from Celle, Germany, and was eventually president of the Lutheran Church—Missouri Synod.

The features of this story are lived out over and over again in millions of lives: the pain of leaving, the ordeal of passage, the risks of new beginnings, networks of immigrant communities, the church helping newcomers, the communal joys and hardships, the spiritual tug of the homeland, the determination to improve the lives of loved ones, the comfort of songs sung and prayers spoken in new and old languages. This experience calls us to the ministry of hospitality toward our immigrant neighbors today.

Lutherans Come to America

Among the earliest settlers in the Americas were Scandinavian, Dutch, and German Lutherans. The Lutheran churches in Europe did not set out to establish religious colonies in North America. Rather, those individual settlers who were Lutheran brought their faith with them. Already in the eighteenth century, Germans—Lutherans among them—had settled in Pennsylvania and the Carolinas. Numerically, the largest migrations of Lutherans took place in the nineteenth century, with large German and Scandinavian communities getting established in the Midwest. The legacy of those immigration patterns is still visible today. The five states with the largest population of Lutherans are Minnesota, Wisconsin, Pennsylvania, Illinois, and Michigan.[2]

In the 1600s, Lutherans were among the early settlers of some of the colonies that later became the United States. Beginning in 1638, the New Sweden colony brought Swedish and Finnish Lutherans to the Delaware Valley. Some of their congregations, such as "Old Swedes" in Philadelphia and Trinity in Wilmington, still exist today—but are no longer Lutheran. After the New Sweden colony was taken over by England, the Swedish settlers and their offspring spoke less and less Swedish and more and more English. They wanted to worship in English, but the Church of Sweden could not send them English-speaking pastors. So they turned to the Anglican Church, and these congregations are now among the oldest Episcopal churches in the United States.

This story illustrates a challenge that the church has faced many times since, and one that is very much present today. People want to worship God and hear God's word in their own language, but how can the church reach out to newcomers who speak a different language from that of the pastor and existing congregation members? And how, if worship has been established in the immigrant language, does the church minister to the offspring and their families who speak English while at the same time ministering to the dwindling number of those who still speak the language of the home country?

The oldest congregation in the ELCA is First Lutheran Church in Albany, New York, established in 1649. This congregation traces its roots to the Dutch and German Lutherans who settled in the Hudson River Valley when that was part of the New Netherlands colony. Another early ELCA congregation is Frederick Lutheran Church in St. Thomas, Virgin Islands. The Virgin Islands were a Danish colony that became part of the United States in 1917. Lutherans in the Virgin Islands are mainly African American descendants of slaves. Already in the 1600s and early 1700s, Lutheran mission work with African Americans began in the Virgin Islands, New York, and New Jersey and with American Indians in New York and Pennsylvania. The inspiration to share the gospel, at least at times, overcame the deep prejudices of race, culture, and language.

In the 1700s, a new wave of German immigration began, especially through the ports of Philadelphia and Charleston, South Carolina. The German immigrants began forming

Lutheran congregations in Pennsylvania. Augustus Lutheran Church, Trappe, Pennsylvania, built in 1743, is the ELCA's oldest unaltered church building. In 1748, the Pennsylvania Ministerium was organized under the leadership of Henry Melchior Muhlenberg and others, becoming the first organized North American Lutheran church structure. All its early meetings and work were done in the German language. Muhlenberg's son Peter followed him in the ministry but gave up the cloth during the American Revolution to become a general in the Continental Army. He later served as a United States senator. Henry Melchior Muhlenberg, an immigrant Lutheran pastor, is revered today as a patriarch of American Lutheranism. His son Peter became a leading patriot and elected official.

The nineteenth century saw large waves of European immigration to the United States, Lutherans among them. Some people made the serious and difficult decision to leave their countries and cross the ocean in order to escape crushing poverty. Others felt stifled by rigid social systems in which enterprising individuals could not advance. Still others wanted to escape religious or political persecution. And there were some who simply wanted adventure. America was an attractive destination because of the availability of land, jobs, and liberty. Immigrant life could be very hard, but there was great opportunity for economic advancement. And without a state church, people could worship freely.

The pattern of Lutheran migration is not surprising. Each group from each country tended to go to places where others from that group had gone before. Church structures followed the patterns of immigration. Many Lutheran church bodies were established, defined by the language of the immigrant group, the region of the United States to which they had come, and yes, sometimes by distinctive theological tendencies. Thus there were Swedish, Norwegian, Danish, Icelandic, Slovak, and Finnish churches (and sometimes several of each), as well as German synods in Pennsylvania, Virginia, North Carolina, South Carolina, Maryland, Ohio, Missouri, Iowa, New York, Texas, Wisconsin, and other states. The longer each group was in the United States, the more they grappled with how to relate to the English language, each one eventually becoming English-speaking. The various Lutheran groups also began tentatively reaching out to other Lutherans, as Lutherans in the United States gradually began to see their Lutheran identity as stronger than their ethnic identity.

A dramatic migration of Lutherans to the United States in the nineteenth century resulted in the founding of the Lutheran Church Missouri Synod. Under the leadership of Martin Stephan, a pastor from Dresden, a group of more than six hundred immigrants from Saxony sailed from Europe in winter, arriving in New Orleans on January 5, 1839. They traveled up the Mississippi, settling in Perry County, Missouri. This group, which included six clergymen and candidates for ordination, left Germany for religious freedom. They objected to the religious Rationalism being propounded in the German church and to the forced union of Lutheran and Reformed churches in some of the German principalities. These Saxons encountered not only the hardships of starting a new life in a new country with an unfamiliar climate and difficult soil. They also found that their leader Stephan was of questionable morals. The Saxon settlement nearly floundered.

Fortunately, one of the other pastors rose up to be an astute, energetic, principled, and inspired leader. Carl Ferdinand Wilhelm Walther became pastor of the first Lutheran church in St. Louis in 1841. He was instrumental in moving the Saxons' school from Perry County to St. Louis in 1850 (it became

Concordia Theological Seminary), and started a German-language church periodical with wide circulation. Joining with pastors from Franconia, Bavaria, sent to America by Wilhelm Loehe of Neuendettelsau in 1847, Walther was one of the founders of the German Evangelical Lutheran Synod of Missouri, Ohio, and Other States—what is now the LC MS.[3]

A sober reality of nineteenth-century migration to America is that the individualism and independence that characterized the choice to leave the old country behind and settle in America usually resulted in immigrants leaving church ties behind as well. Only a minority of those who came from Lutheran countries joined a church on this side of the Atlantic—under thirty percent of Norwegians, not over twenty percent of Swedes, only about fifteen percent of Germans, perhaps twelve percent of Finns, and seven percent of Danes.[4] The eight million Lutherans in the United States today make up less than three percent of the nation's population. If the offspring of all those who immigrated to America from Lutheran lands were Lutheran, that percentage would be far higher.

The great wave of European immigration to the United States peaked just before World War I. During the war, travel from Europe was difficult if not impossible for most. Within the United States, anti-German prejudice put great pressure on Lutheran churches that still worshiped in German to switch to English. A kind of accelerated integration took place. Between the wars, Lutherans continued to migrate to the United States but in less significant numbers.

People Helping People

Throughout the cycles of migration to the United States, people helped each other out. Usually that assistance was informal, with families helping families, people from the same areas helping others from those areas, and so on. But gradually some of the assistance became more formalized.

In what the ELCA history timeline describes as the roots of the Lutheran Immigration and Refugee Service, the New York Ministerium decided in 1861 to start a ministry to protect Lutheran immigrants, especially at the Port of New York. By 1862 the Pennsylvania Synod had agreed to join this ministry, and the Rev. Robert Neumann, formerly a missionary in China, undertook the work. The General Council, a cooperative Lutheran body, was organized and took on oversight of the immigrant work. The Rev. William Berkemeier zealously sought the establishment of an institution in which immigrants could find lodging. The building at 26 State Street was purchased in 1873, and served for twenty-five years to house 227,035 guests. Over thirty-three thousand were lodged without pay, and 20,270 were furnished with free meals, from total contributions of $17,615 for emigrant mission and $10,390 "for poor immigrants."[5]

Lutheran Immigration and Refugee Service was formally established in 1939 under the National Lutheran Council to help resettle Lutherans fleeing from the Nazis. After World War II, LIRS played a major role in opening the doors of the United States to "displaced persons" rendered homeless by the war. More than 57,000 Lutheran refugees were resettled by LIRS in the post-war period from Latvia, Estonia, Hungary, Slovakia, and German-speaking lands in Eastern Europe.[6] Additionally, other Lutherans came as immigrants from Europe but in much smaller numbers than in the 1800s.

After 1965, the United States removed racial and ethnic preferences for immigration from Europe and opened the doors to migrants from other parts of the world. This set the stage for a new wave of immigration to the United States, one we are still living in today. Although the relative numbers have been small, Lutherans have been among the new immigrants. As a result of this migration, in the United States we now find Lutherans from Liberia, India, Indonesia, Tanzania, Ethiopia, Eritrea, El Salvador, Palestine, China, and other countries where the Lutheran church is present. Just like the immigrants before them, these Lutherans were pushed out or pulled in, coming to America for family, for work, for freedom. Additionally, a small but significant number of migrants who were not Lutheran before coming to America have found the Lutheran church here and have been welcomed into it.

{ 3 }

A Nation of Immigrants

The United States is one of the few nations in the world—Canada, Australia, New Zealand, and some of the Latin American countries also come to mind—that understands itself as a nation of immigrants. America celebrates and symbolizes its immigrant heritage with the Statue of Liberty in New York Harbor. Throughout American history, immigration has often been controversial. Indeed, aspects of American immigration settlement have been brutally violent and shameful, most notably the capture, enslavement, and forced migration of persons from the western coasts of Africa and the displacement, disempowerment, and decimation of the Native American peoples.

Yet throughout American history, immigration ultimately has been seen as a positive force, a source of strength, pride, and renewal. Immigration is part of our national identity. This positive sentiment toward immigration is famously expressed in the concluding lines of the poem "The New Colossus" by Emma Lazarus, engraved at the base of the Statue of Liberty:

Give me your tired, your poor,
Your huddled masses yearning to breathe free,
The wretched refuse of your teeming shore.
Send these, the homeless, tempest-tossed to me;
I lift my lamp beside the golden door!

American immigration history can be understood in two
eras—before 1921 and after 1921. Before 1921 the default
position in American immigration law was the open door: anyone could come into the United States *except.* . . The list of
exceptions included those with communicable diseases, con-
victs, prostitutes, lunatics, anarchists, those likely to become
public charges, and Chinese.

Since an act of Congress in 1921 that instituted immigration quotas, the default position in American immigration law
has been a closed door: no one may come into the United States
unless. . . Unless you are closely related to a U.S. citizen or
lawful permanent resident, or you have a work skill needed in
America and there is no American who can fill that job, or you
are a refugee fleeing persecution. All of these criteria work only
when the overall national annual quotas and the country of
origin quotas have not been filled. As one can see, the situation
has become much more complicated since 1921.

The Immigration Era before 1921

In the colonial era, immigration to America was largely unregulated. The settlement of the colonies required hardworking,
industrious people. Compared with the relative abundance of
land and natural resources, people were in short supply and
valued highly. Indeed, some European countries tried to restrict
or even prevent emigration, both to keep their own populations and to prevent the colonies from becoming stronger. Of

course the decision to emigrate was not one to be taken lightly, considering the perils of the Atlantic passage, the dangers of unfamiliar diseases on the American side, and the likely permanent separation from family and homeland.

Even then immigration had its controversies. At several points in his career, Benjamin Franklin wrote about immigration, putting his marvelously inquisitive mind to work on issues that would now be called demography. Franklin was generally positive toward immigration and the need for the colonies to have larger populations. However, he sometimes had questions about certain types of immigrants, especially the large German minority in his home colony of Pennsylvania. He observed that the German immigrants tended to stick together and speak their own language, and he worried whether they would ever integrate into the broader society. In particular, he was worried whether people who came from aristocratically stratified lands and who were at the lower rungs and used to taking orders would ever be able to assert themselves as free people, as full citizens in a free society. Franklin also reveals some racial prejudice in his writings, preferring lighter-skinned Saxons to the other "swarthy" Germans. To his credit, however, he asks whether it is human nature to be more comfortable with other people who more resemble oneself.[1]

The American colonies' positive attitude toward immigration is evidenced in the Declaration of Independence of 1776. The Declaration sets forth a list of twenty-seven of the King of Great Britain's "repeated injuries and usurpations, all having, in direct object, the establishment of an absolute tyranny over these states." Seventh on the list is this:

> He has endeavored to prevent the population of these states; for that purpose obstructing the laws of naturalization of foreigners; refusing to pass others to encourage

their migration hither; and raising the conditions of new appropriations of lands.

Thus the United States of America declared its independence in part to encourage immigration and naturalization.

The Constitution of the United States, drafted in 1787, provides that the Congress shall have the power "to establish a uniform rule of naturalization" Article I, Section 8[4]. The Constitution is silent on immigration; however, given that Article I, Section 8(3) gives Congress the right to regulate commerce with foreign nations, since 1875 it has been well-established in American law that immigration is a matter for the federal government to handle, not the states.

In the early Republic, immigration remained largely unregulated. A notable exception came in the Adams administration in 1798, with the Alien and Sedition Acts, in which Congress authorized the President to expel any alien "dangerous to the peace and safety of the United States." These laws were inspired by fear that the excesses of the French Revolution would spill over to threaten the young United States. They imposed what to modern eyes are shocking restrictions on civil liberties and freedom of speech. The provision cited above expired after two years and was not renewed. After Jefferson defeated Adams and became president in 1801, most of the rest of the Alien and Sedition Acts were repealed.

After the Napoleonic Wars ended in 1815, the first half of the nineteenth century saw a large increase in immigration to the United States. Among the prime source countries were Germany and Ireland, with the result that the Roman Catholic population of America increased significantly. Increased immigration combined with anti-Catholic prejudice led to a backlash strong enough that a political party, the Know-Nothings, included restrictions on immigration as a major part of its platform. A former president, Millard Fillmore, ran on the Know-Nothing ticket in 1856 and carried twenty-three percent of the vote. The party soon collapsed over the issue of slavery.

During the Civil War, it was apparent that immigration was one of the many regional differences that divided North from South. Most immigrants to America had come to the Northern free states. The Southern states, with their more stratified societies, and with slavery so deeply entrenched, did not offer as much opportunity or as warm a welcome to free men and women of modest economic means.

Most immigrants, especially the Germans, were strongly supportive of the Union, and many foreign-born men took up arms for their new nation in the cause of freedom. Almost a quarter of the Union Army was foreign-born. Popular attitudes toward immigrants improved. The Republican Party platform of 1864 declared that immigration "should be fostered and encouraged by a liberal and just policy."

It is notable that one of the major laws passed during the Civil War was the Homestead Act, making federal land available to those—foreigners included—willing to settle and live on the land. Such a law was not possible in a slave state; indeed, before the Civil War, Southern legislators had blocked it. Among those who benefited from the Homestead Act in the Great Plains were many immigrants.

The half century between the Civil War and World War I was the time of the Great Migration to America. Attracted by those same factors of family, work, and freedom, millions of Europeans crossed the Atlantic to start a new life. They came from traditional immigration source countries—Britain, Germany, Scandinavia. In increasing numbers, however, they also came from Eastern and Southern Europe, from Russia and the Slavic lands, and from Italy. An estimated three-quarters of them stayed in America. In the century from 1820 to 1920, more than thirty-three million persons immigrated to the United States, a number roughly equal to the population of Europe in 1800.[2] Throughout much of the nineteenth century, one out of every seven people in the United States was foreign born.

On nearby islands in New York Harbor, two iconic monuments to immigration were established. The Statue of Liberty was a gift from France to the United States, dedicated in 1886. It proclaims America's welcome, the light of liberty. On Ellis Island, America's major immigration inspection and processing station was established.[3] Today, we see Ellis Island as a monument to a successful and welcoming immigration. Remember, however, that its main function was as a screening post. At Ellis Island, newcomers were inspected to see whether they were diseased, indigent, politically dangerous, or otherwise excludable. Those who passed the screen were sent on into America. Those who did not were detained until they could be deported.

On the West Coast, Chinese men had been recruited to help build the railroads and work in the mines. Japanese followed, many working in agriculture. Their presence was controversial from the beginning. American workers saw them as unfair competition, bringing down wages. Western communities were wary and prejudiced, unhappy about having an element of their population that appeared so foreign, that spoke a foreign language and practiced a strange religion. Legal efforts started almost from the beginning to block the immigration of Chinese women and to restrict Asian immigration more broadly. These efforts culminated in the federal Chinese Exclusion Act of 1882, which blocked the immigration of Chinese laborers. This law was not repealed until 1943, as part of the American alliance with China in World War II.

The Immigration Era after 1921

America's involvement in World War I led to an intense chauvinism in American society in which national pride and the need to mobilize for war mixed with fears of alien traitors and anti-German prejudices. Sauerkraut became "victory cabbage." Street names with "German" in them were changed. In some areas, state and local laws were passed that prohibited the speaking of German in public, even going so far as to prohibit German-language church services.

These fears of the foreigner were compounded after the Bolshevik revolution in Russia. Many Americans worried that foreign-born Communists and Anarchists would attempt to take over labor unions, engage in sabotage, or otherwise undermine the United States in the name of an international revolutionary conspiracy. Adding to this volatile mix was a sense among many longer-established Americans that immigration had gotten out of control, with numbers too high and with too many coming who were too swarthy in complexion and too Catholic or Jewish or Orthodox in religion. These prejudices against foreigners and fears for national security led to a movement to restrict immigration. That movement succeeded in Congress in 1921.

The 1921 immigration law, reinforced in 1924, fundamentally shifted the legal dynamics of immigration. No longer did the law assume that most potential immigrants would be allowed in. It was now assumed that most *would not* be allowed in. Overall limits on immigration numbers were set at levels considerably below those of the previous half-century. Country by country quotas were set, with preference given to those coming from Northern and Western Europe.

The combination of the restrictive new immigration laws, the catastrophic economic decline of the Great Depression, and the travel restrictions of World War II led to a dramatic decline in the numbers of immigrants coming to the United States. In fact, during the Depression there was a net out-migration from the United States.

America's restrictiveness was most shamefully illustrated in the failure of the United States to open its doors more widely to those fleeing from the Nazis after Hitler came to power in Germany in 1933. Yes, some thousands were allowed entry, including internationally renowned figures like Albert Einstein. But many more were turned away. Here is one story:

On May 13, 1939, the Hamburg-America steamship *St. Louis* set sail from Hamburg bound for Havana, Cuba. On board were 937 passengers, mostly German Jewish refugees. They were among the last to receive official permission to emigrate, and they had to leave all their possessions in Germany, confiscated by the Nazi government. Many of the men had been released from concentration camps on the condition that they leave Germany. When the ship arrived at Havana two weeks later, it was refused permission to dock. The Cuban president had revoked landing permits for any more German refugees. After five days of fruitless negotiations, the president personally ordered the captain to leave, and the steamship company ordered him to return to Hamburg. Unwilling to return the refugees to concentration camps, the heroic captain sailed north along the Florida coast, making urgent requests that the United States grant asylum. The State Department replied that the German quota was filled and there was nothing they could do. The *St. Louis* was eventually allowed to land in Antwerp and the refugees were allowed entry to Belgium, Britain, France, and the Netherlands. After Germany invaded France and the Low Countries, most of the Jews were taken to concentration camps. Only 240 of the *St. Louis'* passengers survived the war to tell their story.[4]

In the first years after World War II, the doors of the United States remained nearly closed to those displaced by the violence and persecution in Europe. There's a Lutheran parallel to the *St. Louis* story, thankfully with a happier ending:

> During World War II, the small Baltic nation of Estonia was invaded by the Soviet Union, which annexed it, then by German forces, then again by the Soviets. In August 1947, a group of 48 Estonians landed in Miami. They had crossed the Atlantic in open fishing boats. Five Miami Lutheran congregations took them in. However, the U.S. Immigration and Naturalization Service promptly charged them with "irregular entry," detained them, and brought them to Ellis Island for internment. Lutheran church leaders appealed to the INS and to President Truman to grant them asylum. When these appeals failed, the American Lutherans approached their Canadian Lutheran counterparts. Through their intervention, the Canadian government granted entry to the Estonians. In January 1948 these early "boat people" were resettled in the Kitchener/Waterloo area of Ontario. Within five days, the Canadian Lutherans provided them with housing and jobs.[5]

Finally, in 1948, in response to Christian and Jewish religious leaders' appeals to President Truman and the Congress, the Congress passed the Displaced Persons Act. This law allowed entry into the United States of up to four hundred thousand European refugees—"displaced persons" or "DPs"—who had been forced from their homes because of the war. This was part of an international effort to find refuge for all European World War II refugees. Some were integrated into their countries of refuge, such as Germany, Sweden, and Austria; many were resettled in third countries such as the United States, Canada, Australia, and several South American countries. In order to qualify for entry into the United States, sponsors had to guarantee housing, employment, and support. Lutheran Immigration and Refugee Service was the leading sponsoring organization for Lutheran DPs, especially those from Latvia and Estonia. All in all, U.S. Lutherans helped resettle some fifty-seven thousand DPs through LIRS.

Meanwhile, on the southwestern border, immigration controls were much more relaxed. There had been relatively little immigration from Latin America and the Caribbean. Indeed, the laws of the 1920s did not set quotas for immigration from the Western Hemisphere. For generations, persons living in the U.S.-Mexico border region had gone back and forth with hardly any controls, for shopping, for work, for visiting family and friends. The U.S. Border Patrol was not established until 1924, with a contingent of forty-five men to guard the nation's eight thousand miles of land and sea borders. Serious border enforcement did not begin until after World War II.

It had become common for Mexican workers to come north for a season or a year, then to return to their homes and families in Mexico. Sometimes they stayed on the American side, blending in easily and without attracting much attention from the U.S. authorities. Under one of the post-Civil War amendments to the U.S. Constitution, their U.S.-born children became citizens at birth (Fourteenth Amendment, Section 1). There was a similarly relaxed regime on the northern border with Canada. Americans and Canadians could cross back and forth with simply a driver's license, and often they were not inspected at all. Canadians who decided to stay could also blend easily into America.

More Changes—1965 to the Present

American immigration law changed in a major way in 1965. In one of the lesser-known laws of the civil rights era, with strong political leadership from President Johnson and Sen. Edward Kennedy, the Congress did away with racially discriminatory national preferences, the preferences from the 1920s that favored immigration from Northern and Western Europe. In their stead were set up equal country-by-country quotas, as well as strong family unity preferences. The impact of the 1965 law has been to dramatically increase immigration from Latin America and Asia. The face of America has changed as a result.

In April 1975, Saigon fell to the North Vietnamese and Viet Cong forces, and the government of South Vietnam collapsed. Cambodia and Laos also came under Communist control. People on whose side the United States had fought in Southeast Asia began fleeing in the thousands and tens of thousands. Despite political polling that showed that a majority of Americans wanted nothing more to do with Vietnam or the Vietnamese, President Ford felt strongly that the United States owed them a debt of honor. Mustering support from the religious community, labor unions, and veterans groups, he was able to convince the Congress to pass a special law allowing entry to Southeast Asians. In the thirty-plus years since, the United States has admitted more that 1.2 million refugees from Vietnam, Cambodia, and Laos. From the beginning, Lutheran Immigration and Refugee Service has been a major partner in this national humanitarian effort. Again, the face of America was changed through immigration.

The experience of Southeast Asian resettlement, combined with the unsatisfactorily slow and ad hoc responses to the flight of refugees from Hungary, Cuba, China, Uganda, and other countries, made it clear that the United States needed to regularize its law relating to refugee protection. With bipartisan support, the Congress passed the Refugee Act of 1980. The United Nations definition of a refugee was incorporated into U.S. law: "refugee" means any person who is outside any country of such person's nationality and who is unable or unwilling to return to that country because of persecution or a well-founded fear of persecution on account of race, religion, nationality, membership in a particular social group, or political opinion. Under the authority of the Refugee Act, the United States has set up an orderly system for resettling refugees admitted from overseas, as well as for adjudicating the claims of another group of refugees—asylum seekers—who make their own way to the United States and then seek protection here.

From 1975 through 2008, the United States resettled 2,779,000 refugees. In other words, nearly one out of every hundred people in the United States is a refugee. From the beginning, LIRS has been a major partner with the government in this effort, mobilizing the involvement of Lutheran social ministry organizations, congregations, and individuals.

In the early 1980s, it became apparent that U.S. immigration law was not working well. The rigid congressionally defined quotas on how many persons could enter the United States, and for what reasons and from what countries, were not responsive to the supply and demand dynamics of immigration. In short, many people who wanted to come to the United States for family, work, or freedom could not get authorization to do so. Many American families could not unite with their loved ones, and many American employers could not find the workers they needed from the pool of those already in the United States. As a result, by the mid-1980s, there were as many as six million persons estimated to be living in the United States without legal immigration authorization. Something had to be done.

In 1986 Congress passed a law that, on the one side, sought to deter future unauthorized presence in the United States by requiring employers to determine that those they hire have proper documentation proving that they are authorized to work in the United States. (This is the I-9 form that everyone has to sign when they start a new job.) On the other side, the Congress granted amnesty to undocumented immigrants who were already present in the United States, providing they could show that they had been in the U.S. since January 1, 1982, and had a clean criminal record. Some 1.4 million people took advantage of the amnesty and legalized their status. (The INS had estimated that between two and four million might apply.) The 1986 law, however, failed to set up a mechanism to adjust future immigration quotas up or down depending on immigration supply and demand. Thus within a few years, the undocumented population in the United States began to rise again.

The decade between 1986 and 1996 saw the Congress taking some measures that were expansive of immigration and others that were restrictive. The 1986 law included the somewhat quirky "visa lottery," by which persons from countries that were under-represented in current immigration flows could apply to enter the United States without regard to preferences. In 1990, this program was institutionalized as the "diversity visa" program. The 1990 law also significantly increased annual quotas for the number of immigrants, and provided for Temporary Protected Status (TPS) for persons from countries suffering from persecution, war, or natural disaster.

In 1996, faced with growing popular concern over illegal immigration and the sense that the United States was losing control of its borders, Congress on the one hand protected legal immigration—"Keep the front door open"—while on the other hand adopted much sterner measures aimed at punishing and deterring illegal immigration—"Close the back door." The stern measures of the 1996 laws included:

- removing even legal immigrants from eligibility for most federal social welfare programs (as a result, the only major programs for which non-citizens—documented or undocumented—are eligible are public schooling and emergency health care);
- greatly increasing the number of criminal acts for which a permanent resident can be deported;
- eliminating almost all relief from deportation for permanent residents convicted of a crime;
- providing for expedited removal of persons at the border who do not appear to be eligible for entry;
- expanding detention of asylum seekers whose cases are being adjudicated and of non-citizens who are awaiting deportation;
- providing three- and ten-year bars to re-entry for persons who had been unlawfully present in the United States.

As a result of the 1996 Congressional action, there is very little mercy left in American immigration law and very little discretion for an immigration judge with respect to deportation—even for persons whose unlawful entry or whose criminal offenses were long ago and who since have kept their noses clean and become rooted in the community.

After the attacks of September 11, 2001, the Congress passed a number of security laws. The Homeland Security Act of 2002 established the Department of Homeland Security. As a part of this law, the Immigration and Naturalization Service was taken out of the Department of Justice, dismantled, and placed into the new Department of Homeland Security in three pieces: Citizenship and Immigration Service (CIS), Customs and Border Protection (CBP), and Immigration and Customs Enforcement (ICE). One of the results of this new governmental structuring is that immigrants and immigration issues are now seen more and more as security and enforcement issues. Officially, as part of our national effort to protect our homeland security, the positive contributions brought by the overwhelming majority of immigrants are overshadowed by caution and suspicion of the foreigner.

Over the past twenty years, as the number of undocumented persons in the United States has reached record levels, and as immigration enforcement efforts have had mixed success at best, it has become more and more apparent that our nation's immigration law is broken and needs to be fixed. However, the debate is so polarized that major Congressional efforts to achieve comprehensive immigration reform collapsed both in 2006 and 2007. The next chapter will examine the ways in which our system is broken.

{ 4 }

The Current Immigration Debate
and Our Broken System

Despite the long and generally proud history of immigration in America, and despite ours being a "nation of immigrants," we are now in a time of intense controversy over immigration. America's immigration system is clearly broken. The Pew Hispanic Center estimates that twelve million people—one out of every twenty-five people in the United States—are living here without legal immigration status. The issue has become so emotional, so politically toxic, that despite Presidential support, the Congress has been unable to pass a comprehensive reform.

Why is immigration so controversial? Four key factors are record numbers of immigrants, the changing face of America, post-September 11 security concerns, and—most importantly— erosion of the rule of law.

Record Numbers of Immigrants

America is now living through a new Great Migration, comparable in scale to that of a hundred years ago. The Census

Bureau estimates that in 2007 there were approximately 38.1 million foreign-born persons in the United States. With the total population of the United States at just over three hundred million, the foreign-born represent 12.6 percent of the total, or one out of every eight persons in America.

The total number of foreign born is at a historic high. However, the current proportion of the foreign born is not—at least not yet—at the historic levels of a hundred years ago. Between 1860 and 1920, the proportion of the foreign born in the population ranged between thirteen and nearly fifteen percent. The peak was 14.8 percent recorded in the census of 1890, with 14.7 percent recorded in the census of 1910.[1]

The past generation has seen a dramatic growth in the number of immigrants and the proportion of the foreign born. For the four decades, from the mid-1920s to the mid-1960s, immigration to America was at historically low levels. This was due to a combination of factors. On the supply side, the restrictive immigration laws of 1921 and 1924 drastically narrowed the legal immigration door to America, and during World War II civilian travel was virtually impossible. On the demand side, during the Great Depression there was little economic opportunity to attract newcomers. By 1970 the proportion of foreign born in America had declined to 4.7 percent, possibly the lowest level in the history of the Republic. Thus the increase in immigration over the past forty years has seemed even larger when compared to this smaller base.

The Changing Face of America

One of the civil rights laws of the 1960s was the immigration law of 1965. This law removed the de facto racial quotas that gave preference to immigrants from northern and western

Europe. In their stead was enacted a preference for family reunification and equal country by country quotas. The consequence of the 1965 law has been a dramatic increase in immigration from Latin America and Asia, and to a lesser extent from Africa. As a result, over the past forty years the complexion of America has become much more diverse. We see this in almost all our communities. Just think about how many Asian and Mexican restaurants there are, and how few there were forty years ago.

Furthermore, partly as a result of immigration and partly as a result of lower birth rates among whites, America's race dynamics are changing in a profound way. America's racial make-up is no longer the classic majority white, minority African American. The population of Hispanics in the United States recently surpassed that of African Americans. The Pew Hispanic Center estimates that by 2050, at current rates of population change, whites no longer will be a majority in America. This has already occurred in the largest state, California.

The increase in immigration in general, and the increase in immigration from non-traditional source countries in Latin America and Asia in particular, has unsettled many native-born Americans. Who are these newcomers? What about their strange languages and customs and religions and appearance? Will they integrate? Will they speak English? Will they bring the conflicts of their home countries with them? Will they adopt American democratic values?

It should be noted that these questions are nothing new. Remember what we said about Benjamin Franklin. These questions raise the same concerns that Franklin raised about the integration of the Germans in colonial Pennsylvania. He complained that they stuck together, spoke their own language, and were not imbued with democratic values. In one sense,

Franklin was right—Pennsylvania did indeed change because of the Germans being there, making their contributions, and helping shape their new homeland. But Franklin was wrong in that over time most of the Germans (the notable exception being the Amish) adopted English, embraced democratic values, intermarried with others, and fully integrated into American society. This dynamic of immigrant integration into American society and culture is basically the same today, even if the countries of origin are different.

Security Concerns since September 11

Since the horrible and shocking attacks of September 11, 2001, America has become more fearful and less secure. The nineteen hijackers who carried out the attacks were foreigners who had entered the United States on temporary visas, either as students or as visitors. Even though they were not immigrants, the immigration debate has been strongly affected by their actions. Do we have control over our borders? Do we really know who is in our country? How do we know whether the foreigners who are here mean us well or mean us ill? How can we make sure that other terrorists do not infiltrate our country? Until these questions are resolved to our satisfaction, many Americans will be suspicious of immigrants and skeptical about proposals for comprehensive immigration reform.

Erosion of the Rule of Law

In our view, of all these factors, immigration is most controversial because of the erosion of the rule of law. There are an estimated twelve million persons living in the United States who are here without legal immigration status—one out of every twenty-five people in America. Americans think of themselves as a law-abiding people living in a nation under law, an orderly place where people follow the rules. They do not like to be taken for chumps, to feel that there are certain people who are getting unfair advantages as a result of skirting the law. Radio talk show hosts ask, "What part of illegal don't you understand?" It bothers us that immigration law is violated on such a massive scale. The system is broken and it needs to be fixed. But it is terribly difficult for Americans and our Congress to agree on a solution. In the meantime, the brokenness of the law becomes more and more frustrating.

Most immigration law violations are civil in nature rather than criminal. Other examples of civil violations include speeding and parking tickets. Civil violations do not imply the same degree of harm to public order or moral turpitude that criminal violations do. Legally speaking, they are not as serious. In the popular mind, however, illegal immigration is identified with crime. If it is illegal, it must be criminal, and "illegal immigrants" must be criminals.

Since 1996, Congress has contributed to that identification by drastically reducing the legal possibilities for those who are here without legal immigration status to stay. Previously persons who had been in the United States for a certain number of years without status could stay here if they had clean criminal records and had put down ties in the community. Now such relief is exceptionally rare.

In addition, Congress has made it easier to deport even lawful permanent residents who have committed crimes, even if those crimes were committed long ago, the person had already served their time, and the person had become a law-abiding member of the community since then. The penalty for an immigration violation—deportation and the resultant tearing apart of families—appears to be more and more disproportionate to the underlying damage to public order caused by unlawful presence.

Might the immigration situation in America today be comparable to that of Prohibition in the 1920s and early 1930s? America then had a national law (a Constitutional amendment even) prohibiting the manufacture or sale of alcoholic beverages. The law was violated on a massive scale. A large proportion of Americans did not agree with the law and saw nothing morally wrong in drinking. Enforcement resources were poured into efforts to uphold Prohibition, with no apparent effect. Indeed, Prohibition created an environment for the growth of criminal enterprises and eroded respect for the law. Eventually, Prohibition was repealed and the manufacture and sale of alcoholic beverages was regulated in a more reasonable and workable way. Sometimes it is better to fix a broken law than keep trying to enforce it in ways that are more costly to society than the underlying harm the law is trying to prevent.

How Is the Immigration System Broken?

We discussed earlier the reasons people come to America—for family, for work, for freedom. Our current immigration system is broken in all three of these areas.

Family

In one sense, America is generous in receiving foreigners who want to reunite with family. The basic rule is that U.S. citizens are able to sponsor their spouse, unmarried minor children, and parents without regard to visa limits. This area of family unity works reasonably smoothly. Beyond that there is a limit of 226,000 visas per year for family-sponsored immigrants, and the visas issued per country are subject to annual country-by-country quotas. With respect to family visas, preference categories are (in descending order of preference): adult unmarried children of U.S. citizens, spouses and minor children of lawful permanent residents (LPRs), adult unmarried children of LPRs, adult married children of U.S. citizens, and siblings of U.S. citizens.

Nearly two-thirds of lawful immigrants are admitted in family categories: In 2006, 1,266,264 foreigners obtained lawful permanent resident—"Green Card"—status in the United States. Of these, 45.8 percent were an immediate relative of a U.S. citizen, and another 17.5 percent came through a family-sponsored preference, for a total of nearly eight hundred thousand persons admitted to join their family. Yet even though these numbers are large, the system is rigid and does not respond to the demand for family unity. Here are several examples.

Lawful permanent residents—Green Card holders—who want to be reunited with their spouse or minor children, must sometimes wait years to do so if their spouse or minor children were not admitted at the same time they were. In October 2008, the State Department was processing such visa applications that were filed on January 1, 2004. For citizens of Mexico, however, the national quotas are oversubscribed and the applications being processed in 2008 were filed on May 1, 2001. This means that the lawful permanent resident from most countries must wait at least three years and nine months to be reunited with his or her spouse. If the LPR is from Mexico, he or she must wait seven years and five months. Is there any public policy benefit to be served by an immigration law that keeps husbands and wives separated for years and years?

Imagine that you and your spouse are U.S. citizens of Philippine origin. You are getting older. Your daughter is a Philippine citizen who is unmarried—she is widowed and living alone. She would like to come to the United States to care for you. In October 2008, for most countries, the State Department was processing visas for adult unmarried children of U.S. citizens that were filed on April 15, 2002—a six and a half year wait. However, the national quota for citizens of the Philippines is oversubscribed, and the applications being processed were filed on April 1, 1993. So your daughter can come care for you, but she will not be able to arrive until fifteen years from now.

The final example is that of a Lutheran woman from New Jersey, a U.S. citizen of Guyanese origin. Her brother is developmentally disabled and was being cared for in Guyana by their mother. Their mother died and there was no one else in Guyana to care for the brother. The sister applied for her brother to come to the United States so she could care for him. The immigration authorities agreed but said they would have to wait eleven years for the visa to come current. Today the waiting time for visas for siblings of U.S. citizens is still eleven years. Fortunately, the brother had a visitor's visa. He came to New Jersey to visit his sister. When the visa expired, he stayed on, thus becoming unlawfully present in the United States. The sister kept caring for him. When the eleven years passed, the brother was able to pay a fine and adjust status to permanent residency. Was it morally wrong for the sister to care for her brother and for him to be unlawfully present in the United States? Or is it the working of the law that was immoral? The provision of the law that allowed for persons to adjust status when their visas become current has since been repealed by the Congress. Today the brother would have no legal way of staying in the United States.

Work

The mere fact that there are an estimated twelve million persons unlawfully present in the United States shows how broken the immigration system is when it comes to work. In 2006 the United States admitted approximately 160,000 lawful permanent residents through employment-based preferences for principal applicants and their dependents. This falls far short of demand. Large sectors of the economy—primarily in construction, agriculture, services and hospitality—cannot find enough native-born workers and depend on immigrant labor.

The number of legal visas issued each year is fixed by Congress and does not go up or down depending on the demands of the U.S. economy. For many years now, the supply of legal visas has fallen far short of the demand for foreign workers. These powerful economic forces have resulted in large-scale employment of undocumented workers, despite the employer sanctions imposed by the 1986 immigration law. Indeed these economic forces are so powerful that each year thousands of Mexicans and Central Americans risk their lives being smuggled into the United States through the Sonoran Desert in Arizona. Tragically each year hundreds of them do not make it and die an excruciating death in the desert.

In her 2006 article in *Foreign Affairs*, "Immigration Nation," Tamar Jacoby noted that the Bureau of Labor Statistics reckons that between 2002 and 2012 the U.S. economy will create some fifty-six million new jobs, half of which will require no more than a high school education. More than seventy-five million baby boomers will retire in that period. Declining native-born fertility rates will be approaching replacement level. Native-born workers, meanwhile, are more educated. Jacoby writes: "Arguably the most important statistic for anyone seeking to understand the immigration issue is this: in 1960, half of all

American men dropped out of high school to look for unskilled work, whereas less than ten percent do so now." Currently, the demand for unskilled jobs that is not being filled by native-born workers is between 400,000 to 500,000 per year. Yet under current law, the annual number of immigrant visas for unskilled workers is only five thousand.[2] The law is broken.

Freedom

The United States is the most generous country in the world in admitting refugees for resettlement, taking in more than half of all refugees resettled worldwide. The scale of this generous welcome is illustrated in that from 1975 through 2008, the United States resettled 2,779,000 refugees. That means that nearly one out of every one hundred people in the United States is a former refugee. In addition the United States admits asylum seekers—refugees who make their own way to this country to seek protection from persecution. Millions of persons who have been forced to flee from their homes leave everything behind have found new hope and new life in America.

However, the immigration system is also broken when it comes to freedom. From 1975 to 2000, the United States admitted on average ninety thousand refugees for resettlement. After the attacks of September 11, refugee resettlement was shut down for several months while all the security screens and protections in the system were reviewed and enhanced. The resettlement system was then gradually brought back into operation but still has not returned to prior admission levels. Average admissions from 2002 through 2008 have been only forty-four thousand per year, half the historic levels.

Legal and political factors have contributed to these lower resettlement numbers. As part of the USA Patriot and Real ID

Acts, Congress barred entry to the United States to persons who had provided material support to terrorist groups. That is perfectly reasonable on its face—no one wants supporters of terrorists to come into the country. The problem, however, is that the definition of "material support" did not include an exception for support given under duress, and the definition of terrorist group included any two or more persons who take up arms against an established government. Under these definitions, Jews who paid bribes to the Nazis to escape from Germany in the 1930s would be barred entry to the United States, and George Washington and the Continental Army would be considered a terrorist group. It has taken considerable effort to get waivers to allow legitimate refugees to overcome the material support bars to entry, and these efforts still have a long way to go.

The primary political challenge to refugee resettlement has been with regard to Iraqi refugees. Since the U.S. invasion of Iraq in 2003, the United Nations estimates that more than two million Iraqis have fled the country and another two million plus have been forcibly displaced within Iraq. The United States has proven reluctant to admit Iraqis for resettlement—for security reasons, in order to make sure that terrorists do not plant themselves among those being admitted, and for political reasons, so as not to give up hope that the security situation within Iraq will improve enough that refugees can return home safely. In the meantime, in 2007 the United States admitted only 1,608 Iraqis for resettlement; in 2008, the number was just over 12,000.

A final illustration of the system's brokenness is the detention of asylum seekers. Under the 1996 anti-terrorism laws, persons who enter the United States seeking asylum who do not have proper immigration documents are held in immigration detention facilities while their identity is verified and their asylum claims are adjudicated. This includes vulnerable persons such as victims of torture. In effect, persons who flee persecution and come to America seeking liberty are locked up while we figure out what to do with them. The overwhelming majority of these asylum seekers pose no threat to society or to themselves and could be monitored through means far less drastic than imprisonment.

The Suffering Caused by the Broken System

Since the collapse of immigration reform efforts in Congress in mid-2007, the offices of the Evangelical Lutheran Church in America in Chicago and Lutheran Immigration and Refugee Service in Baltimore are getting more and more calls from pastors and church members about the fear and suffering caused by our broken immigration system. After reform efforts collapsed, the Bush administration increased the level of interior immigration enforcement, increasing the number of workplace raids on employers suspected of having undocumented workers. No one expects these raids to be successful on their own. Even at the increased level of raids and deportations, it would take centuries to apprehend and deport all of the twelve million undocumented. The theory behind the increased raids is "enforcement through attrition"—raising the level of risk and of fear—so that the undocumented will decide it is no longer worth it to stay in the United States and will go home on their own.

Typical of the calls to the ELCA and LIRS is the situation of a family in which a parent who is undocumented has been apprehended and is facing deportation. The other spouse may or may not be undocumented as well—it is not uncommon to have families in which one spouse has legal status and the other does not. Under current immigration law, it is virtually impossible for the undocumented spouse to regularize status and remain in the country. It is quite common that some or all of the children in such families may be U.S. born, and thus citizens under the Fourteenth Amendment to the Constitution. The Pew Hispanic Center reckons that in 2005 there were 3.1 million U.S. citizen children living in families with mixed immigration status. Seventy percent of the undocumented are in mixed-status families.

The mixed-status family, in which one parent is facing deportation, faces a terrible dilemma. After the one parent is deported, should the family live apart? Current immigration law provides that a person deported will not be allowed to reenter the United States for at least ten years, if then. Or should the rest of the family uproot themselves to join the deported family member, assuming that the country to which the parent has been deported will allow entry to the rest of the family? This is a terrible decision for a family to have to make, and it creates a difficult role for the pastoral counselor trying to assist them. More and more mixed families are living in fear that one parent will be deported and they will have to face such a choice.

From a public policy perspective, it is not at all clear that the public interest in enforcing the immigration laws through deportation outweighs the harm to the family, especially to the children. In the case of a U.S. citizen child, the current enforcement regime results either in the child living separated from his or her parent or, if the child follows the parent being deported, in exile as a U.S. citizen.

The cost of enforcing the broken immigration law falls not just on those being deported and their families. It falls on their communities as well. The immigration raid in Postville, Iowa, on May 12, 2008, provides a vivid illustration. The ICE raid on Postville targeted the employees at AgriProcessors, Inc., the nation's largest kosher meatpacking plant. Federal agents said they were investigating known violations of immigration law on the part of the company, including keeping separate lists of undocumented workers. Union organizers also alleged wage and labor violations, such as paying undocumented workers less than the minimum wage, employing underage children, and making threats of retaliation against workers who complain. The 389 persons detained in the raid were all workers; none were management. More than three hundred of them have been charged with crimes relating to identity fraud around false or improper Social Security numbers. Later in the year, several supervisors and the company itself were charged with violations of immigration, workplace safety, and child labor laws.

The impact on the community has been devastating. The population of this little town in northeastern Iowa had fallen to eight hundred before the meatpacking plant came in. The population grew to 2300 as the town overcame adjustment challenges, arriving at a healthy diversity of Anglo, Orthodox Jewish, and Hispanic residents. Then on May 12, fifteen percent of the town's people were arrested and taken away. In the resulting climate of fear, half of the town's schoolchildren were absent the following day, and more than two hundred persons sought refuge at St. Bridget's Catholic Church, afraid to return to their homes. According to one of the sisters at St. Bridget's, some children are wondering if they will ever see their parents again. The ELCA designated Postville as a "domestic disaster," the first time an immigration incident has been so designated.

The Rev. Steven L. Ullestad, Bishop of the ELCA North-eastern Iowa Synod, and a graduate of Postville High School, shared his personal experience with the raid carried out in his hometown:

> May 12th happened and everything changed. That morning, schools and computers were shut down. All the roads into and out of Postville were blockaded by people with guns and guard dogs. Government trucks crashed through the gates of the local meat packing plant. Hundreds of ICE officers and other police officers in flak jackets with guard dogs and guns surrounded the place. Everyone with Latino background was brought out in handcuffs, whether they were documented or undocumented, while Black Hawk helicopters with machine guns visible circled overhead. Our little town of 2300 was in shock. One local pastor described it as an invasion. The archbishop used the word 'terror' to describe the impact on the community. One woman asked the question of me, "Why did the government decide to destroy our town?" I need to emphasize the number of people—389 individuals arrested in a town of 2,300—that are simply gone. You can imagine the impact on families, schools, downtown businesses, and everything else. Why do this to towns and why do this to children?[3]

Fear spread throughout the community, not just among the undocumented and their families. Young schoolchildren whose parents are Americans were traumatized when their classmates disappeared, and they wondered if their own parents would be arrested and taken away. You cannot uproot people from a community without wounding the whole community.

Beyond families and communities being torn apart and the increased climate of fear in immigrant communities, another pain caused by the broken immigration system is the increased ugliness of the debate, the hateful and offensive language that is used against immigrants in general and Hispanics in particular. Is it becoming socially acceptable in America to say such hurtful and discriminatory things?

In September 2008 several Lutheran bishops met with Rep. Zoe Lofgren (D-CA), the chair of the House Immigration Subcommittee. Rep. Lofgren is herself a Lutheran and an immigration lawyer, the granddaughter of a Swedish immigrant who had little education and little English but who worked hard and provided for his family. It is a tribute to his efforts that his granddaughter became a member of Congress.

Rep. Lofgren reflected on how difficult it is to find common ground in the immigration debate now, in part because so much of the anti-immigrant language is becoming harsh and dehumanizing. The worst recent example, she said, was when her committee was debating a bill to offer immigration benefits to the families of American military personnel killed in action. It was proposed to name the bill after the first American soldier killed in the Iraq war, Marine Lance Cpl. Jose Gutierrez, who happened to have been an immigrant from Guatemala. One of the anti-immigrant Congressmen objected, saying, "Do we know if he was legal?" Apparently, immigration status was more important than the ultimate sacrifice that soldier made for America. Rep. Lofgren went on to observe that things that now would be completely unacceptable if said about African Americans seem to be said freely about Hispanics. She asked with dismay, "Can people say anything about Latinos in America now?"

Until there is comprehensive immigration reform, there will be more and more license in America to denigrate and divide and treat certain groups of people as being less than equal, less than worthy. It does America no honor to have an underclass living in fear and subject to insult. The broken immigration system needs to be fixed.

{ 5 }

A More Just Future:
Four Spiritual Values

Over the years, as Lutheran Immigration and Refugee Service has evaluated various proposals for reform of the immigration system, it has settled on four criteria to weigh whether the reform proposal looks promising or not. When we reflect on why it is that these criteria have served us so well for more than half a decade now, we realize that it is because the criteria are firmly grounded in spiritual values. The four questions we ask are:

- Does the proposal promote family unity?
- Does the proposal promote human rights and worker rights?
- Does the proposal enable those without status to come out of the shadows and live without fear?
- Does the proposal provide a path to permanence as a full member of society?

These questions provide a clear framework for the moral evaluation of both present and proposed immigration policies.

Does the Proposal Promote Family Unity?

Family unity has always been a cornerstone of both U.S. immigration policy and of immigration related advocacy by many faith-based groups. This is not surprising, because we are all born into families. Throughout human history, the family has been the first and most important protector of human life and wellbeing. The Universal Declaration of Human Rights recognizes this when it states: "The family is the natural and fundamental group unit of society and is entitled to protection by society and the State" Article 16[3]).

As it represents the Lutheran churches in the immigration debate, LIRS's "advocacy will continue to insist that family reunification should be the primary objective of immigration laws." As described in the previous chapter, the current backlog of family preference visas makes U.S. citizens and legal permanent residents wait up to fifteen years or more to reunite with their families. Comprehensive immigration reform can ensure that family unity policy is strengthened, both for undocumented people who receive permanent status and for immigrant and refugee families already in the system—some of whom are waiting in the shadows here, others of whom are waiting in their home countries.

Family Values in the Bible

In most Christian traditions the family is the place where personal identity is formed in light of justice, mercy, compassion, forgiveness, and the like. The family is a sacred place of caring, nurture, and love. Family values, keeping the family together or reuniting the family, are at the heart of our position regarding any proposed immigration reforms. The story of Jesus' presentation in the temple (Luke 2:21-32) gives us wonderful images of loving parents fulfilling their spiritual obligation for their child and of the open, outstretched hands of an old man in the community of the faithful poised to receive and hold the baby.

> Now there was a man in Jerusalem whose name was Simeon; this man was righteous and devout, looking forward to the consolation of Israel, and the Holy Spirit rested on him. It had been revealed to him by the Holy Spirit that he would not see death before he had seen the Lord's Messiah. Guided by the Spirit, Simeon came into the temple; and when the parents brought in the child Jesus, to do for him what was customary under the law, Simeon took him in his arms and praised God. . . . (Luke 2:25-28)

Focus on the hands of an old man, the hands of a grandpa. And think about the hands of the mother. Father David Garcia is the pastor of San Fernando Cathedral in San Antonio, Texas. He described how his Mexican American community celebrates the Festival of the Presentation. At the heart of the celebration are the hands of the mother, "La Virgen de la Candelaria," the Lady of the Candles. In one hand she holds a lighted candle, in the other the Christ child. Themes of epiphany light and the presentation of Jesus in the temple come together.

At the presentation Candelaria Mass, the priest blesses three things brought from home to church by the people. He blesses the candles used at home altars for family devotions. Then he blesses the "ninos," which are the Christ child figures from crèche scenes. And then the priest blesses the infants and children gathered there. The connections between the altar table and the kitchen table, between the Christ child and all children, between the church and the home and the world are beautifully woven into the celebration of the presentation. Here is the richness of parish and family life.

The presentation of Jesus flows from the incarnation of Jesus, the word taking flesh in the world, in a family. Consider the incredible richness of parish and family life symbolized in the presentation story in the Gospel of Luke. In the presence of Jesus and his parents, and his growing extended family in the temple, we call for immigration reform that protects precious families and keeps them together.

Does the Proposal Promote Human Rights and Worker Rights?

Migrant workers come to the United States so they can work, and they find dignity in their labor. But all too often they also experience lower wages, exploitative labor practices, dangerous working conditions, and constant fear and insecurity. Providing legal documents for honest, hardworking migrants would discourage such abuses of human rights and worker rights.

Many immigration reform proposals include provisions for an expanded migrant worker program, predicated on the idea that such workers will come to the United States for a limited period of years and without the expectation that they will permanently settle here. As we evaluate such proposals, we urge that they include two key rights provisions. The first is arguably the basic worker's right—the right to quit your job. This right separates employment from servitude. It protects the worker from exploitation, because the worker has the freedom to quit if working conditions are intolerable or if there is a better opportunity. In the immigration context, promoting this right would mean that the migrant worker's visa would be tied to the worker rather than to the employer.

The second key rights provision is the right to live in one's family. Migrant workers should have the opportunity to have their close family members join them in the United States, and they should be able to leave and reenter the United States to visit family members who have chosen to stay in the home country.

Human and Worker Rights in the Bible

The Hebrew people in captivity in Egypt had neither human nor worker rights. The Hebrews were slaves. They could not quit their work. They were exploited and abused like a group of deaf and mute undocumented young people from Central America who were held in virtual slavery in a Jackson Heights apartment. These "los muditos" were forced to sell trinkets on subways and beaten if they did not make their quota or tried to. Their undocumented status made them vulnerable to exploitation. They stayed in virtual slavery because they had no legal status and easily could be jailed and deported back to the hunger and poverty from which they came.

We have met Fujianese workers held in slavery until they paid off their debts, incurred to buy transportation to America. Asian and Eastern European young women are part of the global sex trafficking that renders them slaves. Philippine and African domestic workers have been held as slaves for years in the homes of wealthy folks from their own country now living in America. Where there is no legal document, there is abuse, broken families, and indentured workers without rights or recourse.

The word Hebrew means "those who have withdrawn to the margins." Moses came upon the abuse of one of his fellow Hebrews (Exodus 2:11-12). The text says that "he looked this way and that," and "seeing no one," he killed the Egyptian persecutor. When we first encountered this story in Sunday School, we were taught that, after looking around, Moses saw that the coast was clear. Rabbi Hillel, a contemporary of Jesus, had a different interpretation. Hillel wrote that Moses was *looking for help*, and that the rest of the Exodus narrative is about how Moses was never again in the position of looking this way and that and finding no help. The Exodus narrative was about the creation of community, *a solidarity based on justice, grounded* in the compassion of God. The Hebrews left Egypt a motley crew. They entered the promised land a people, bound together in Yahweh, the God of widows, orphans, and the oppressed. The God of the strangers among us (see Deuteronomy 10:17-19).

The story of the stranger is our story; we are a nation of immigrants, all of our roots go back to the experience of being a stranger in a strange place. Our immigration situation today calls for solidarity on behalf of the stranger, especially when our new neighbors are abused, denied their basic rights, find their families torn apart and their lives in virtual slavery. When we look this way and that, will we find one another in the community of Jesus?

Does the Proposal Enable Those without Status to Come Out of the Shadows and Live without Fear?

The vast majority of the twelve million undocumented people living in the United States are otherwise law-abiding, honest, hard-working people who want to provide for themselves and their families. While the United States has the sovereign responsibility to control its borders and enforce its immigration laws, it must also create migration policies consistent with its constitutional and humanitarian values. Newcomers without legal immigration documents are among the most vulnerable for whom we are called to care. By bringing people out of the shadows of fear and marginalization, we allow our immigrant communities to live in the light of liberty, contributing more freely to our culture and economy. Moreover, by better documenting who is in our country, we can strive for smart enforcement, fair proceedings, efficient processing, and targeted enforcement against those who want to harm us.

Those without Status and the Bible

The gospel turns things around and upside down. Christ has "broken down the dividing wall" (Ephesians 2:14), and we now know that all the racial, economic, class, and gender distinctions we use to divide are no longer relevant (Galatians 3:28). We all have equal status at the table as beloved children of God. The words of the Apostle Paul are instructive on the nature of the table of the church and its relation to those without status and living in fear. While imprisoned in Rome, Paul "a prisoner of Christ Jesus" writes to Philemon and to "the church in [Philemon's] house" about Philemon's slave, Onesimus, who has been in Rome caring for Paul.

> I am appealing to you for my child, Onesimus, whose father I have become during my imprisonment. Formerly he was useless to you, but now he is indeed useful both to you and to me. I am sending him, that is, my own heart, back to you. I wanted to keep him with me, so that he might be of service to me in your place during my imprisonment for the gospel; but I preferred to do nothing without your consent, in order that your good deed might be voluntary and not something forced. Perhaps

this is the reason he was separated from you for a while, so that you might have him back forever, *no longer as a slave but more than a slave, a beloved brother*—especially to me but how much more to you, both in the flesh and in the Lord. (Philemon 1:1-3, 8-16, 25, emphasis added)

This short letter gives us a fresh look at Paul the Apostle on the run, constructing a mission theology—sometimes messy, sometimes with a lot of loose ends—in the thick of the action. See how he improvises on the authority of the gospel, and his own authority as a servant of the gospel, to strengthen the table. Paul affirms the partnership of many in the work of the gospel. He nurtures the faith, companionship, and gifts of those around the table. And he extends the table toward the world, in this case a fugitive slave. It is what every congregation and Christian is called to do every day.

As in all his letters, Paul lifts up various partnerships in his relational salutation. He reminds them that, wherever they are, they are joined together in the "grace of our Lord Jesus Christ" (Philemon 1:25). Paul is always naming names: "Apphia our sister," "Archippus our fellow soldier." And Paul is always drawing connections between places, in this case his jail and the household table of Philemon. The benediction at the end names more names and places. Paul's apostolic leadership is one bringing to mind the connections, the koinonia of the church, and its inclusion of all God's children.

Paul grounds the partnership, and his particular ministry of bringing Onesimus out of the shadows and back into community, by naming the source of his mission: "Grace to you and peace from God our Father and the Lord Jesus Christ" (1:3). He sends words of encouragement to strengthen their faith and discipleship. He prays for them, reminds them of their giftedness, and exhorts them in the Christian life: "I pray that the sharing of your faith may become effective when you perceive the good that we may do for Christ" (1:6). This is Paul the missionary. He addresses his congregation about their life together. Like the best preachers who claim a pulpit for God, he expects the public reading of his letter; it is written not just to Philemon but also to "the church in your house" (1:2). There is table business to discuss, and it is public business.

We take a similarly bold stance in our advocacy for immigrants without status, living in the shadows. Paul is appealing for Philemon to place a seat at the table for Onesimus, the slave who is a fugitive from Philemon's house but who has served Paul in his imprisonment. Paul calls this slave his own son, just as Jesus called the outcast woman with the twelve-year hemorrhage "daughter." What would it mean today if we called illegal aliens sisters and brothers, sons and daughters?

Christian congregations and leaders see transformed relationships and name them. Onesimus was a slave, but now he has a seat at the table as a brother. Paul is teaching us table manners. Philemon is called to treat Onesimus as a partner in the work of gospel. He must see Onesimus with new eyes, no longer a slave but a *beloved brother*. They are now kin, tablemates. As Paul so profoundly put it in Galatians 3:28: "There is no longer Jew or Greek, there is no longer slave or free, there is no longer male and female; for all of you are one in Christ Jesus." The gospel transforms relationships, status, even the economics and politics of the household and community.

So must we respond in our own time, with a hospitality that transcends the labels that divide, that create suspicion and fear, that strip away the dignity that all deserve as children of the God who calls people out of darkness into light.

Does the Proposal Provide a Path to Permanence as a Full Member of Society?

Throughout its history, a great strength of the United States has been its welcoming of immigrants, manifested by the desire and expectation that immigrants will become citizens and fully participating members of civic society. This tradition means that the United States has avoided having a permanent underclass of people of foreign origin who do not share the same rights and thus are subject to discrimination and exploitation. Any immigration reform should provide a path to permanent status and citizenship for persons who put down roots in America and want to become contributing members of society.

A Path to Permanent Inclusion and the Bible

To be included, to have a permanent place at the table, is the dream of all immigrants, a dream that often goes unrealized. The biblical story of Ezra opening the book of the law of Moses and blessing the Lord before the Water Gate in Jerusalem's walls is a beautiful narrative of what it looks like when a people comes home (Nehemiah 8:1-3, 5-6, 9-10). The path to permanence is through the believer's heart. Israel had been in captivity and exile, and those who remained in the ravaged land had been living in the shadows. Their lives had been at risk, they were not at home in captivity in Babylon; they grieved and found it difficult to worship in a foreign land. In their transient life as immigrant exiles, Jeremiah called them to pray: "Seek the welfare of the city where I have sent you into exile, and pray to the Lord on its behalf, for in its welfare you will find your welfare" (Jeremiah 29:7). The vast majority of immigrants, both documented and undocumented, seek the welfare of their new land, trusting that in its welfare they will find their welfare.

The Hebrews would know that they were home when they could gather and worship the living God in their own language. "For surely I know the plans I have for you, says the LORD, plans for your welfare and not for harm, to give you a future with hope. Then when you call upon me and come and pray to me, I will hear you (Jeremiah 29:11-12). That promise was being fulfilled. They had rebuilt the walls of their shattered city. They had gathered at the Water Gate. In this great assembly they heard the word of the Lord spoken in their own language, and they heard it with understanding. They wept for joy. A part of their worship was to welcome the stranger and welcome the poor by "sending portions for whom nothing had been prepared" (8:10). They were home. The exile path led to a permanent dwelling.

Permanent Inclusion among Us

When the pastor and leaders of Salem Lutheran Church in Bay Ridge, Brooklyn, handed the keys, the check book, and the registry of the congregation and its 103 years of pastoral acts to Pastor Khader El-Yateem and the leaders of newborn Salaam (Peace) Arabic Lutheran Church, a people in exile received a path to permanence and full inclusion. Here were free and faithful Lutherans from two very different cultures sharing immigrant roots, taking the time and supreme effort to fall in love with another set of table companions. Salem was the Water Gate for the people of Salaam. A path to permanence and inclusion is not just a legislative value but a spiritual gift.

The folks at Salem said, "Take care of our heritage," and the folks at Salaam replied, "The church you cared for is in good hands." These brothers and sisters had walked together through the pain and exhilaration that comes from letting go of the familiar and comfortable and being grasped by the transforming power of the gospel.

Their experience reminds us that every congregation must be ready to surrender the church of their past in order to be open to the church of God's future. The church stands at the "Water Gate" declaring the word of God to the exile, to the alien, to the stranger among us. While Christians in this country "eat the fat and drink sweet wine," they are called to share the gifts of this land with "those for whom nothing is prepared." We understand this call in the light of God's promise to Abraham and Sarah: "I will make of you a great nation, and I will bless you, and make your name great, so that you will be a blessing . . . and in you all the families of the earth shall be blessed." (Genesis 12:2-3).

{ 6 }

Putting Our Feet on the Road
in Mission

Joy Dryfoos, in her book *Adolescence at Risk: Prevalence and Prevention,*[1] analyzes many programs in use among adolescents in cities aimed at such issues as alcohol and drug abuse prevention and treatment, crime, job training, and self-esteem. Among those programs deemed successful, she identifies many different factors that account for the program's success. Her top two factors are the quality of justice and the quality of mercy. Each successful program required the effective collaboration of all the institutions in the community that touch the child's life. The programs produced real social change in institutional relationships on behalf of the child. Each successful program also employed one-on-one relationships between adolescents and caring adult mentors.

The church's mission to and with our new immigrant neighbors must follow a model where justice and mercy flow together. We need both individual and collective means of engagement. In this chapter we share approaches to this mission in the hope that you will be inspired and challenged to join what God is already doing in your community and nation to welcome the stranger. An intentional response by the church to our growing immigrant population and the broken system addressing it in our country must be an integral part of the overall mission of the church. Every congregation is a mission station. Every pastor is a mission director. Every baptized child of God is a missionary in the world. Every congregation's mission includes service and ministry to immigrants.

Synods and national church bodies exist to inspire, resource, link, and accompany congregations in their mission. The direction of this mission is not inwardly focused on the church but outwardly focused on the world, the nation, the community, the neighborhood. The heartbeat of mission is the worship of God's people—the altar, the pulpit, the baptismal font, and the people of God gathered around word and sacrament. Justice and mercy for the life of the world is the Lutheran response to our changing America.

Hospitality and Invitation

"His dog barks loudest" is a supreme compliment in the Arab world. Strangers on the road are welcomed with radical hospitality whenever they appear. The barking dog noticing the approaching visitors is the first sign of hospitality for wandering strangers.

In the story of Abraham by the oaks of Mamre, three strangers approached Abraham's tent (Genesis 18:1-8). His reflexive response was not to check their credentials or size up their intent but to lay on the feast. In so doing, he unwittingly entertained angels and provided hospitality to God.

Pastor Gemechis Buba is the Director for African National Ministries for the Evangelical Outreach and Congregational Mission unit of the ELCA. He has helped to plant over one hundred ministries to African immigrants. Most of these ministries have taken root in existing congregations, examples of radical and holy hospitality. These African immigrant missions are vibrant and exciting communities, but they have not been formed simply to create ethnic enclaves in America. They are formed for mission in their new communities.

Pastor Buba has developed training materials for Lutheran congregations titled "Initiating and Facilitating Cross-Cultural Missional Hospitality." At the heart of this training is the biblical witness to hospitality as a foundational spiritual stance. Pastor Buba lists the many biblical accounts of radical hospitality and identifies the spiritual rhythm of mission that shapes these accounts: invitation, hosting, and sending. We invite the stranger in, become the host, and eventually the stranger becomes one of us, sent out in the ministry of hospitality. Lutheran engagement in immigration issues should not begin with policy discussions or arguments but with the practice of hospitality. First we welcome the stranger, then we work with them to address our broken immigration system.

We cannot give hospitality until we get in touch once again with our own experiences of receiving hospitality. That is why it is so important to remember our own families' immigrant experiences, and to listen to the birthing stories of our own congregations. It is also why visiting companion synods or other places in the world where we have partners in the gospel is so important. Such visits can be a profound experience of being welcomed, of being vulnerable in a strange place, of being the stranger at the table.

Repairers of the Breach: What Congregations Are Doing

Isaiah 58 is a powerful prophetic message addressed to the community of Israel who had returned from exile in Babylon. They had resumed their religious practice in Israel. They called upon God, they worshiped and fasted but felt that God was paying no attention to them: "Why do we fast, but you do not see? Why humble ourselves, but you do not notice?" (Isaiah 58:3). God's answer to their complaint goes to the heart of Israel's (and the Christian church's) existence. God commands them to "loose the bonds of injustice, to undo the thongs of the yoke, to let the oppressed go free, and to break every yoke." God is apparently not interested in religious rites, rituals and practices *unless* they are accompanied by justice and mercy. The prophet Amos also conveys the message that festivals and assemblies are not pleasing to God unless the community also lets "justice roll down like waters, and righteousness like an ever-flowing stream" (Amos 5:24).

Jesus agreed with Isaiah and Amos. Once, when scolded by the religious leaders of his day for not following the food and cleanliness laws by eating with "tax collectors and sinners," he replied: "Go and learn what this means, 'I desire mercy, not sacrifice'" (Matthew 9:13; cf. Matthew 12:7). It would seem that our worship, our fastidiousness about religious rules and rituals, does not sit well with God if we are not deeply engaged in the struggle for justice and mercy. But if justice and mercy top the agenda of God's people, then Isaiah makes it clear that things will go well with God's people. We will be repairers of the breach (Isaiah 58:14), able to heal the tears, ruptures, violations, and estrangement we find all around us.

Many "breaches" in contemporary American society call out to God's people for repair: the broken immigration system and the desperate lives of millions of both documented and undocumented immigrants; the plight of political asylum seekers and refugees; the suffering of those incarcerated for coming to this country without proper documentation; the estrangement between citizens and non-citizens. Healers of the breach are found everywhere in the ELCA, as well as in our ecumenical and interfaith partners. Some recent immigration ministries of the Metropolitan New York Synod and the Southwest Texas Synod are serving "in the breach" in powerful ways. Similar ministries are taking place throughout the ELCA.

Huntington Lutheran Respite Center

In Suffolk County, Long Island, anti-immigrant violence has been particularly prevalent. Among the many incidents of violence are the beating death of a Mexican immigrant lured to a phony construction job and the death of an Ecuadoran immigrant beaten to death by a gang of high school youth out looking for a Latino to attack. Deacon Richard Thydon and other members of Gloria Dei Lutheran Church in Huntington Station saw migrant workers sleeping in the woods and decided to act instead with compassion and hospitality. Members of Gloria Dei organized the Huntington Lutheran Respite Center. A network of hosting congregations provides shelter, serves a hot dinner and breakfast, and gives a lunch and hygiene kit to those they host. A food pantry and used clothing shop have been organized.

Ascension Lutheran, Deer Park

Pastors Al Triolo and Dennis O'Roarke took their church into the breach when they walked the neighborhood, talked to a variety of immigrants, and decided to call a Latino pastor to begin an outreach to the Spanish-speaking community. With no other congregation reaching out to the rapidly growing Hispanic community in Deer Park, Ascension has taken the lead by bringing Pastor Plaza onto its pastoral team. The pastor and other leaders and members continue the practice of walking the streets of Deer Park, sharing the love of Jesus and listening to the needs of the people in the neighborhood.

Jorje Ospina and St. Luke's Lutheran, Woodhaven, Queens

Jorje Ospina, a carpenter from Colombia, began a Spanish-language outreach at St. Luke's, ministering to the huge influx of mostly South America immigrants in Woodhaven, Queens. St. Luke's originally reached out to German immigrants but had declined to the point where its future was in doubt. The decline might have to do with the congregation losing touch with its changing community. The ministry to South American immigrants is now revitalizing the mission of the parish.

The partnership between Pastor Ospina and the English-speaking pastor has been effective. They share the basic duties of the parish, with Pastor Ospina taking primary responsibility for seeing to the spiritual and material needs of the immigrant population. Most of those St. Luke serves in its neighborhood outreach are undocumented. Pastor Ospina carves small crosses and hands them out at the local Laundromat where he prays with the people and invites them to St. Luke's. Immigrants serving immigrants has been a tremendous blessing to the Lutheran community in New York.

The Sparrow Finds a Home: Detention Watch

The church is both home and refuge, a place where men and women and children find comfort and safety, nurturing and nourishment, a place where the dignity of the children of God is shared by all. The ancient Hebrew poet said it well: "Even the sparrow finds a home, and the swallow a nest for herself, where she may lay her young, at your altars, O Lord of hosts, my King and my God" (Psalm 84:3).

Lise Kitoko is a fifteen-year-old child of God from Congo. She fled Congo when her entire family was taken away by government troops for being supporters of deposed President Mobutu. With the exception of her mother, they are all presumed dead. Her mother had gone ahead to Canada to seek asylum, and Lise was on her way to Toronto to meet her. At JFK airport she was questioned by INS officials and given a dental test, on which basis they claimed she was an adult. They put an orange jump suit on her and threw her into the Wackenhut detention center near Kennedy Airport. This is essentially a jail for refugees in waiting, including children.

When the church met Lise, she was very depressed, had no one with whom she could speak, and had lost weight because she has been unable to eat regularly. She is a Christian but had not been offered spiritual counsel or the opportunity to pray. It is hard enough being a fifteen-year-old girl under normal circumstances. She was spending twenty-three hours a day locked up with no windows.

The church met Lise in the breach. The Metropolitan New York Synod's East African ministry at Our Savior Lutheran Church in Jamaica, Queens, along with LIRS and Lutheran Community and Family Services, gave personal and sustained attention to Lise Kotoko. This attention included public advocacy for Lise and for other asylum seekers. It included regular visits from Pastor Perucy Butiku, the leader of the East African ministry, and members of the Swahili and Lingala speaking Lutheran community. They prayed, comforted, and shared spiritual nurture and hope with Lise. And they agitated for Lise's release. With every visit, the light of truth and justice broke into that insulting place and kept the pressure of God's grace in the breach. This ministry accompanied Lise to her hearings, interceded on her behalf, and sponsored her during the asylum seeking process.

The authorities moved Lise to the Elizabeth, New Jersey, detention facility in an attempt to escape from these annoying Lutherans who would not let her, her warders, or the system that incarcerated her alone. Those annoying Lutherans found her and visited her in the Elizabeth detention facility. Finally the immigration authorities set Lise free to join her mother. This was public ministry at its best, with Lutheran and ecumenical communions working as a team. It began by showing up, seeing what was happening, and then taking action to bring justice and mercy into the breach. It continues to happen every day across the country as Lutherans continue to show up in detention centers as "repairers of the breach," people with a shared vision of a better dwelling place in their hearts and prayers.

Pastor Ruben Duran, an immigrant from Peru, works in the mission of the ELCA as Director of Mission Starts for the Evangelical Outreach and Congregational Mission Unit of the national church. The first time he came to America he found himself incarcerated. When he tells his immigration story, he makes two things clear. "First, my story is about what lies beneath the surface. What you see is not necessarily what you get. There are so many myths about immigration. The immigration officers saw in me a burden, but God turned it into a blessing. Second, one little question from one person can become a door for God to act."

Ruben learned about the Lutheran church from LCA missionaries in Peru. He became a youth minister and was encouraged to continue his theological and vocational formation in Seattle at the Lutheran Bible Institute. Many in Lima raised funds for his trip and education. As he entered the United States in Miami, it was discovered that there was a $500 gap between what he needed to enter the country and what had been raised. It made his Form I20 inadequate for entry, and he was placed in the detention center in Miami.

Ruben remembers being interrogated by an INS officer every hour as he waited deportation on the next flight to Peru, leaving twelve hours later. He remembers his sense of shame at the thought of returning home defeated after the whole community had gathered to send him off with such high expectation and hope. He questioned himself and his faith. At one point an officer asked him sardonically, "Just what do you think you are going to study anyway?" Ruben said, "This book," as he took out his Bible. He said the officer looked at it and then in a kind of exasperated tone said, "Go. Get out of here." And he was free to continue his journey in America.

Be Not Afraid

Jesus said, "Be not afraid!" In response to immigration enforcement that breaks families and communities apart, LIRS and the ELCA have set up a program by that name. Be Not Afraid is a pilot project designed to equip congregations to respond to immigration issues impacting their members and communities. Congregations are fractured over the issue, not sure how to respond as the family of Christ. Pastors are confronted by enforcement officers, the loss of members, and declining participation in classes and activities. Immigrant families are fractured by a broken system that often denies due process, separates parents and children, and creates a culture of fear impacting daily life. Be Not Afraid wants to turn back the fear and inspire people with strength and hope. It focuses on four critical areas:

- be informed: Provide presentations and materials for immigrants and their families;
- be equipped: Provide training and resources for congregations and volunteers;
- be prepared: Network congregations and partners for ICE raid response as needed;
- be an advocate: Provide resources for those interested in advocating for better policies.

As a result of the Be Not Afraid pilot, congregations will be better equipped to discuss faithful responses to immigration issues, respond proactively to the needs of immigrant members and neighbors, and be more engaged in their communities through outreach and service.

The New Sanctuary Movement

Rev. Carlos Paiva, of Angelica Lutheran Church in Los Angeles, looked up near the furnace in the basement of his church and noticed a sign on the wall. He dusted it off and read: "Sanctuary, 1980." It recalled a time almost thirty years ago when that congregation hid undocumented neighbors from Guatemala in the basement of the church. One hundred years ago, Angelica's role in that community was to be a blessing for the Swedish immigrant community. That sign from the past reminded Pastor Paiva that "God has placed us in the community we are in right now to be the hands, eyes, ears, heart, and soul of Jesus in this place. One of the issues right now is the Latino, Korean, and African immigrants in our community. We listened to the people and we decided to be a New Sanctuary Movement site."

The key concept of the movement is "prophetic hospitality," building on the biblical tradition of hospitality discussed earlier in this chapter. In much the same way that congregations have sponsored refugees over the years, congregations will publicly provide hospitality and protection to a limited number of immigrant families, whose legal cases clearly reveal the contradictions and moral injustice of our current immigration system while working to support legislation that would change their situation. Host congregations sign a "Sanctuary Pledge," and other supporting religious leaders and congregations also sign onto the pledge. Thus a conference or a ministerium or a synod could support individual congregations willing to engage in this ministry. There are strict criteria for families to be hosted. They must

- be engaged in the legal process and under an order of deportation;
- have children who are U.S. citizens;
- have a good work record;
- have a viable case under current law.

They will be families like that of Yolanda who came to the U.S. from Guatemala in 1989. For four years she had "Temporary Protected Status," which allowed her to work in the United States and establish a life without fear of deportation. Her status expired due to an error on the part of her attorney. As a child, Yolanda was orphaned. She has a deep fear that if she is deported her daughter will go through a similar experience. Yolanda is a deacon at her church, where she also serves in the food pantry and as a leader in the women's association.

In the New Sanctuary Movement, the congregation becomes home base for the family. The congregation is their mailing address and a place to spend time as needed. Sometimes this means that housing is provided by the congregation through its members. The congregation and its partners provide both material and spiritual support for the family. Expert immigration lawyers handle the case. The congregation is public in its support and joins with its partners and New Sanctuary Movement members from across the country to help lift up the human rights of immigrant families as children of God.

Local Acts of Mercy

Sometimes congregations do what comes naturally to the body of Christ and reach out to help the most vulnerable. Sometimes that person is an undocumented immigrant. It was three years ago that Zuleica Arano and her mother Lucinda Estrada began knocking on the doors at churches in their suburban Chicago neighborhood. They were trying to raise money for transplant surgery for Zuleica who was in the end stages of renal disease and near death. They were immigrants without documents or money, and no hospital would deal with them.

The desperate woman in Matthew's Gospel reached out to Jesus and was able to clutch the hem of his garment, not thin air (9:19-22). He was there to be touched, in her path, in her community. And when she touched him, Jesus saw her, a person, not an outcast, a pariah, or an alien. "Daughter," he called her. Jesus transformed this anonymous encounter into a relationship. Strangers become kin in Christ. And there is more in this encounter. The woman grasping the hem of his garment is not only needy, ill, and a ritual outcast. She is also gifted. He sees it and names it: "Your faith has made you well." For Zuleica and her mother, the hem of Jesus' garment was the door of Living Lord Lutheran Church, and the pastor who opened it, Rev. Jean Duran (Ruben's wife). "My heart really went out to them," she said of that encounter and the story she heard.

A partnership was formed between Living Lord and Church of the Holy Spirit, a nearby Roman Catholic church. Together they set out to raise $150,000 and began a series of fund raisers. "We sold everything we could think of," said Sister Marianne Supan, pastoral associate at Church of the Holy Spirit. Other churches and community donors pitched in. Pastor Duran says, "It was wonderful to have all these churches working together for this lifesaving cause." Zuleica's successful surgery took place in September of 2008, and it turned out that her mother was a perfect kidney donor for her. Both are home from the hospital and recovering. They were strangers, "illegal aliens," until someone saw them through the eyes of Jesus.

Take heart, mother. Take heart, daughter. Remember that Jesus was on the way to the house of a desperate father whose daughter was dying when his garment was grasped by a desperate woman on the road. The question for the church is how to place the hem of Christ's garment where it can be grasped by those caught up in our broken immigration system. Sometimes we take the first step on the road simply by answering the door. In the name of Jesus, answer the door.

{ 7 }

Standing in the Breach

Many Lutheran congregations actively welcome the stranger and provide caring, supportive ministries of service to immigrant populations. They have discovered new life within their communities of faith as they struggle to be faithful to the gospel of God's love by embracing these new neighbors through ministries grounded in love and justice. They have been renewed and revitalized through the many gifts they have received from the immigrants they have welcomed. Here are some of their stories.

Agape Asian Ministry—ELCA

La Crosse, Wisconsin
Interviewee—Houa Moua

French fur traders named the settlement La Crosse. A congregation of thirty-eight Norwegian immigrants created the Lutheran church there. Led by Pastor P. Asbjornsen, they built a place to worship, establish community, and engage in the work of the Lord.

Over one hundred years later, their congregation has continued that work of welcoming the most recent stream of immigrants. Seeing their history in the experiences of the newcomers, St. Paul's Lutheran Church has reached out to the refugees of Laos and Thailand. In their building, Pastor Houa Moua has begun a ministry to the Hmong refugees of La Crosse, creating a Lutheran congregation made up of former refugees. Like the early Norwegians his congregation is small, but through his work Agape Asian Ministry has repeated the pattern of extending a hand to demonstrate God's love for the most recently displaced people. The emphasis rests on *agape*—the Greek word for unconditional, charitable love among brothers and sisters in Christ.

A refugee himself, Pastor Moua converted to Christianity after a missionary came to his village in 1949. Resettled in the United States in the wake of the violence sweeping Southeast Asia, he began preaching in his home until he was called by the La Crosse Area Synod. Ministering in Hmong and English, he has baptized thirty members into Agape. He seeks to reach the Hmong population, only five percent of whom are Christian. He teaches the good news, his faith born out in service.

Through his leadership, Agape Asian Ministry has developed the Agape Planning Project, a collaboration with Catholic Charities and the Hmong Mutual Assistance Association to serve the four thousand Hmong refugees among them. It offers physical support to those in need and provides classes on language, immigration and family issues, and workplace preparation. The congregation sees their role as welcoming the stranger and responds with assistance and support. They have worked for their new neighbors and for the rights of Hmong in Thailand and Laos, collecting 3246 signatures of support. Following the example of Lutherans in the past, Agape has become a place of unconditional love and hospitality.

The Lutheran Church of All Nations—LCMS

Nashville, Tennessee
Interviewee—Jasson Kalugendo

The Greek city of Antioch was the cradle of early Gentile Christianity. If Jasson Kalugendo has his way, Antioch will once again be a beacon for urban churches. This time, however, he refers to Antioch, Tennessee, a former dairy farming community on the outskirts of Nashville. Neither the town nor its minister follows the traditional definition of overseas mission. Beginning his work in his home of Tanzania, Pastor Kalugendo served as a missionary to Sweden and Rwanda before making his way to Tennessee. He saw a spiritual need in America and responded to a call from the Lutheran church to minister to the people of Nashville.

The result is the Lutheran Church of All Nations. The church has grown out of Pastor Kalugendo's work in connecting with neighbors by going from door to door asking "Do you believe in God?" Each encounter takes place within the growing diversity of the neighborhood. He sees the community shifting from blue-collar Americana to a mix of immigrant cultures.

Coming predominately from Southeast Asia and Latin America, the families he encounters speak twenty-three different languages. He hopes to reach them all, reaching out to the youth to build bridges among the majority, minority, and immigrant communities. His excitement spills out as he discusses plans for the church to develop a mission center, a worship center, a media center, a research center—anything to reach people with the gospel. His vision is of a Lutheran church truly embodying all nations, building community, and sharing the word of God.

Bridge of Peace Community Church

Camden, New Jersey
Interviewee—Giselle Coutinho

"What happened to the American Dream?" Pastor Giselle Coutinho regularly hears this question from members of her congregation. She tries to prepare herself for the traumatic and discouraging stories that usually follow it. Most recently it was the story of an undocumented Brazilian immigrant working in construction for $3.50 an hour. When he fell off a seven-story building on the job, his supervisor put him in a cab to the hospital, where he did not immediately receive treatment because no one spoke Portuguese. Pastor Giselle, whose father was Portuguese, came upon him at the hospital and translated for him.

Pastor Giselle serves Bridge of Peace Community Church in Camden, New Jersey, the second poorest city in the country. In this place of material poverty, her church provides a piece of God's grace and aid to the community around it. The church pulls together the marginalized in a congregation of amazing diversity. A quarter white, a quarter black, a quarter mixed race, and a quarter Latino, the congregation is home to many differently-abled children and families with undocumented immigration status.

One thirteen-year-old girl in the congregation whose parents do not have legal status was reading *Anne Frank: Diary of a Young Girl* with the rest of her class. Few of her class-mates felt as strong an identification with the young victim of such hate and violence as she did. The girl was at home one afternoon when Immigration and Customs Enforcement (ICE) agents came to raid her apartment building. Earlier they had taken away her father, so the girl's mother told her to run. Hiding in a steam trunk in the basement, no one could find her. When Pastor Giselle finally uncovered her hiding place, the girl peered out at her and asked, "Why in America do I have to be Anne Frank?"

For all the forgotten faces and hidden lives of the undocumented, Primo Levi's words on the Holocaust ring true: "One single Anne Frank moves us more than the countless others who suffered as she did but whose faces have remained in the shadows. Perhaps it is better that way; if we were capable of taking in all the suffering of all those people, we would not be able to live."

Christ Assembly Lutheran Church—LCMS

Staten Island, New York
Interviewee—Philip Saywrayne

Pastor Saywrayne's congregation worships in a refurbished bagel factory on Staten Island. They move through the aisles, dancing and waving handkerchiefs, singing with their lyrically trained choir. They mingle their traditions from Liberia, Ghana, Suriname, Guyana, and the United States. Much of the congregation fled war and violence, and in the church they find a family and support to begin their lives again. Many have faced great hardship, both in assimilating to the United States and in struggling with the things they have seen. The congregation acts as benefactor and counselor, ministering to the physical and the spiritual needs of each member. One-on-one, they provide true counsel in helping to process the trauma refugees have experienced. They support one another while navigating the maze of immigration policy and social services, waiting in lines together, going to get work permits together. A true community of faith, they are fully present for each other.

They also spread their ministry. As the congregation on Staten Island has grown past four hundred people, Pastor Saywrayne's work has included building new churches all over the Northeast. He listens to God's call, working with the LCMS to direct his mission and skill.

He began his ministry in Liberia and is led by the grace of God, building up leaders and founding eight new churches. This extraordinary evangelism is an outpouring of faith, a response to the Great Commission of Jesus Christ. Faith, through suffering and into joy, has spread into mission.

Christ Lutheran Church—LCMS

Lansing, Michigan
Interviewee—Zerit Yohannes

As they filtered into the mainstream media, heart-wrenching stories of Sudan's Lost Boys caught the conscience of the nation. The members of Christ Lutheran in Lansing, Michigan, were no different. But they were not just hearing of a distant tragedy. Their church was surrounded with a growing community of refugees, mostly from the Sudan.

Not content to be observers, the church organized the Refugee Development Center to bring support for those families whose lives had been shattered by years of war and neglect in refugee camps. The church recognized the difficulty of integrating into a new culture, especially for those who spent all their lives in a camp. Cut off from any culture, either that of their home country or host country, children spent their entire lives in camps. They learned only of war, only of survival of the fittest.

Coming to Michigan, they faced the challenge of relearning how to live in community. The Lutherans of Lansing sought to give them the physical, emotional, and spiritual support that resettlement alone did not bring. They reconciled families whose children assimilated faster and more completely than their parents. They taught language and driving and modern technology. They taught community, as lost children learned to play, have parties, and associate. In so doing, they built a congregation from Burundi, Sudan, Iraq, the Congo (Brazzaville), the Democratic Republic of Congo, Rwanda, Somalia, Ethiopia, Eritrea, Liberia, Cote d'Ivoire, Malawi, Cameroon, and the United States. Pastor Yohannes sees the need as very broad. "We must touch their minds and hearts to exert effort to adjust," he says. It is exactly what he and his congregation have done.

Dallas Oromo Mission—ELCA

Richardson, Texas
Interviewee—Tsena Dinssa

"In our own languages we hear them speaking about God's deeds of power" (Acts 2:11).

For an hour of worship each Sunday morning, the slight, sweet drawl of Dallas, Texas, does not permeate the walls of St. Luke's Lutheran Church. Oromo replaces it, as refugees and immigrants from Ethiopia and Northern Kenya worship in their own language.

The small band of seventeen people who regularly attend Dallas Oromo Mission represent a tiny portion of the five thousand Oromo who live in the Dallas-Fort Worth area, many of whom brought with them a religious heritage deeply impacted by the Lutheran church. Marked, too, by persecution in Ethiopia, the Oromo church has shaped the relationships of its members. Coming to Dallas, their traditions were shaken as people sought to maintain their faith without their language. When Oromo Mission began, members shared their single Oromo Bible, taking up a collection to ship more from Germany.

Dallas Oromo Mission seeks to offer its members their own private Pentecost, where the word of the Lord comes to them in their own language. For Pastor Tsena Dinssa, this is an act of hospitality. Rather than insulating the Oromo church from its English counterpart, worship in Oromo allows it to serve the glory of God and the good of humanity more fully. It is an inclusive gesture of Christian hospitality and love. Already closely connected to St. Luke's, worshipping together one Sunday a month, Oromo Mission has sought to reach Oromo immigrants, helping them to integrate socially through English and immigration classes. They engage with the community and the greater body of Christ as Christians worshipping in their own language.

Immanuel Lutheran/Light of Christ—LCMS

Saint Louis, Missouri
Interviewee—Paul Rueckert

In a way, the Chinese community came to Immanuel Lutheran Church. They moved into the church's neighborhood outside St. Louis, started families, and built lives. They saw

Immanuel and were curious. Slowly, they made connections with the congregation. Although most of Immanuel's members do not live around the church, they saw the changes around it and responded with a ministry, devoting their resources to the creation of Light of Christ Chinese Mission. It has thrived.

The congregations worship together four times a year in Mandarin and English. As they recite the well-loved words of the Lord's Prayer together, the two languages mix with a strange beauty. To Pastor Paul Rueckert, it "feels a bit like Pentecost." As it was at Pentecost, the Chinese members often go out from the church to great struggle. Many members are in St. Louis for only a short time before returning to China, where Christianity is still tightly controlled.

While Chinese members remain in Missouri, they reach out to serve the needs of the larger Chinese community. Beyond Sunday morning service, the Mission provides English classes, driving classes, and faith-based parenting classes, inviting members from both congregations and the broader community. For the members of Immanuel, Light of Christ has been a way to live out their belief that the gospel is for all nations, no matter their race, language, or culture. For the Chinese community, Light of Christ has brought the light of the gospel and a welcome into the community of faith.

Faith Lutheran—LCMS

North Palm Beach, Florida
Interviewee—John Frerking

"We can't help everyone, but we can help one family," Pastor Frerking said in 1975. Like the rest of the nation, the North

Palm Beach pastor was gripped by television images of refugees fleeing Vietnam, people clinging to helicopters in Saigon, boatloads of people hijacked by pirates. Recognizing his capacity to help even a little, he made a few calls and arranged to sponsor a resettled family. Shocked by how easy it was to find them a house and a job, he asked to sponsor another. This prompted a wave of families over the next thirty years, each with its own story, each offered new hope through Pastor Frerking's work and that of his congregation, Faith Lutheran.

Working mostly with Vietnamese, Burundi, and Bosnian refugees, he saw families reunited, families offered homes and livelihood through the generosity of his congregants. He saw men and women coming to faith in response to the Lutheran example of service.

He sponsored a father and three sons who believed their mother and sisters dead. By working with the Red Cross, he found them and reunited the family in Florida. A Burundi woman, welcomed into Pastor Frerking's congregation, said, "Your community has shown me such love. We need the Lutheran church in Burundi."

After a friend of Pastor Frerking's was able to cure a pain in his ear, a Muslim refugee began attending his church. "Here's your Muslim Lutheran again," he would say, never forgetting the aid that he had been given. A Bosnian family, previously sponsored by the congregation, took the role of welcoming a newly arrived Serbian family.

But for all his work, Pastor Frerking sees himself as benefiting more than anyone. In the refugees he helped, he saw the Lutheran values he learned as a child. He saw the values of family, work ethic, and education that American culture often lacks. Refugee families provided a model of thankfulness, loyalty, and generosity. America needs their example. Through them, he saw the hand of God, the promise that the smallest act of love bears fruit.

Latvian Evangelical Lutheran Church—LELBA

Washington, D.C.
Interviewee—Anita Varsbergs Paza

Hunched over a round table, several small, blond heads nod with intense concentration over the stack of eggs and bright paints in front of them. This is a common scene on many Easter mornings in Washington, D.C., but these children chatter to each other in rapid Latvian. Their egg painting takes place in the Latvian Evangelical Lutheran Church of Washington, D.C., a church committed to a community of Latvian Christians.

The congregation began over fifty years ago as a ministry to Latvian Lutherans fleeing poverty or Communism who entered the D.C. area. Since that time, the church has taken on the role of cultural preservation, offering a space to honor heritage and pass on customs. Services and events, extended to the public, are conducted in Latvian. The church also conducts Latvian school on Sunday mornings during the school year, providing a place for children to learn about their heritage in a Christian context. As the Latvian community assimilated into the dominant society of the country's capital, the church continues to provide a place to commemorate, celebrate, and convey culture. It is a space where culture remains alive and present, where church members treasure their ability to worship God through their Latvian heritage.

Trinity Lutheran Church—ELCA

Pelican Rapids, Minnesota
Interviewee—Laurie Skow-Anderson

The meatpacking plant was the reason. When it started hiring Hispanic seasonal workers thirty years ago, the plant introduced the first ethnic diversity to this small Lutheran town of Norwegian dairy farmers in rural Minnesota. Eventually, these positions became permanent, attracting waves of Vietnamese, Bosnian, and Somali families. Trinity Lutheran Church is still adjusting to these dramatic changes in its community of 2400 people.

Struggling to follow Jesus' command to love our neighbors, the church has opened its doors to a variety of programs, slowly but steadily moving out into the community. They have provided for the physical needs of their neighbors; one congregant has earned the nickname the Mattress Man for his ability always to find a bed. Sunday School classrooms are used to hold WIC (Women, Infants, and Children) classes while church members hand out healthy snacks and nutrition information to connect with their new neighbors. During Vacation Bible School, neighborhood children outnumber the children of Trinity members. In the mornings, Scandinavian children play soccer with their Hispanic neighbors and huddle for Bible study in the afternoons. Pass-It-On, a thrift store run by the church, donates thirty thousand dollars a year to local organizations. Through these services, the church is moving through resistance to awareness, understanding, and friendship. Through their new neighbors, church members are learning the differences between Islamic faith and Islamic fundamentalism, everyone taking steps to appreciate difference.

Grace Lutheran Church—LCMS

Winter Haven, Florida
Interviewees—Mildred Bernthal and Jean Wright

The first refugee families resettled by LIRS came to Winter Haven, Florida, in 1976. Airlifted after the Fall of Saigon, the two families had helped the CIA and faced death or imprisonment if they stayed in Vietnam. As the two sisters and their husbands and children left Camp Pendleton, Jean Wright was there to meet them. She and the Women's Guild of Grace Lutheran Church had arranged food, clothing, and housing for these new members of their community. For Mrs. Wright, the newcomers became members of the family, coming together for holidays, weddings, and funerals long after they were resettled. Prompted by Pastor August Bernthal, this initial act of welcome changed the congregation completely.

"It was my husband who resettled all those families," Mildred Bernthal says, praising the extraordinary work of Grace Lutheran in sponsoring over three hundred families. As she raised six children while providing comfort and support for the refugee families, Pastor Bernthal took on more and more advocacy. As the congregation built community around their work, their pastor observed first hand the plight of the refugees. He traveled to camps in Southeast Asia, Africa, and the Philippines, fighting for solutions and compassion.

After observing the horror and crisis of the refugee camps, he would return home to baptize Vietnamese children, to watch men recertify their dental licenses, to encourage students as they graduated from college. The work proved its own reward as strangers became friends and newcomers became family. The congregation reflected this reward, growing from 20 to

2800 under Pastor Bernthal's leadership. It has become a place of astonishing welcome and extraordinary grace.

Iglesia Paz y Esperanza—ELCA

Willmar, Minnesota
Interviewee—Naomi Mahler

One Willmar, Minnesota, Lutheran church's potluck has more than hot dish and Jell-o salad to offer on a Sunday afternoon. Over tortillas at Iglesia Paz y Esperanza, high school students translate Spanish into English so that their parents can understand. Methods of communication stretch beyond the usual easy chatter of church fellowship. Its name means "peace and hope," and in that spirit the church has become a place for dialogue, a partner in service, and a space for community in the midst of a changing neighborhood. It encourages, supports, and aids those working in the Latino immigrant population.

When Pablo Obregon was called to Willmar, his ministry reflected a change in the small Minnesotan town. A seminary student at the time, he responded to the needs of three ELCA congregations. Over their monthly breakfast meeting, the town's pastors decided that Pastor Obregon should extend the ministry to Latino immigrant families who have come to the town.

Growing out of his work, Iglesia Paz y Esperanza has emerged as a bilingual ELCA church serving the Latino community. The church has created a place for mutual exchange as Spanish- and English-speaking people come together to form connections and build bonds.

Pastor Naomi Mahler has found this to be a source of both challenge and strength. It is not easy to be a member of Iglesia

Paz y Esperanza. Church members must work hard to communicate across language barriers, and they must be intentional in building relationships that seek to overcome the fear, uncertainty, and concern that pervade the immigrant community. Amidst the conflict, the church offers peace and hope.

Northfield Refugee Committee

Northfield, Minnesota
Interviewee—Judy Dirks of Bethel Lutheran Church

Minnesota winters do not offer the most hospitable conditions. The frigid shock of Canadian winds that steal all the moisture from exposed skin stands in sharp contrast to the wet warmth of Vietnam. Starting in 1975, however, the churches of Northfield, Minnesota, began a service of hospitality for the waves of refugees that came to America in the wake of the Vietnam War.

Nestled forty-five miles south of the Twin Cities, Northfield offered little protection from the weather. But the congregations worked quickly to welcome the strangers in their midst. Involved from the beginning, the four Lutheran churches in the town of seventeen thousand worked with Methodist, Catholic, Baptist, Moravian, Congregational, and Episcopal congregations to sponsor and resettle refugees. This effort evolved into the Northfield Refugee Committee, which has worked since then to aid the displaced. The ten churches have resettled some one hundred Vietnamese refugees.

Judy Dirks acted as chair of the committee for twenty-four years, befriending, teaching, and learning from these new people around her. Over those years, she has seen the pain of the past, the difficulty of adjusting to English, to winter, to American culture. This pain is tempered by the joy of new citizenship, new homes, new college degrees, and weddings celebrated at Bethel Lutheran Church. Received into Lutheran congregations, the Vietnamese were hungry and fed, thirsty and given something to drink, strangers and welcomed, in need of clothes and clothed, sick and attended. They were in prison and visited. In return, they have given joy to the lives that they have touched. As Judy Dirks describes it, "They have left footprints on my heart."

Pan de Vida Lutheran Church—ELCA

El Mirage, Arizona
Interviewee—Pastor Mitchell Eickmann

Pan de Vida has been a congregation in flux. It has changed along with El Mirage, Arizona, absorbing the shifts in demographics and politics. Through its shifts, it has worked to create a community, to build a family of its members. When Mitchell Eickmann was called to pastor the small Hispanic church, he celebrated his first liturgy with two women and their children on Mother's Day. Since that time, he has welded together a congregation whose people truly care for each other, a congregation that seizes ownership and agency and fights for its existence. Pulling in curious neighbors and wintering seniors, the church has crafted its own Lutheran identity. It has been a tumultuous journey, but a sense of mutuality has become the strength of the congregation.

One little boy started it. A bright-eyed, captivated listener, the third grader was brought to church by a neighbor family vaguely dissatisfied with the direction of the new pastor. The child watched and learned, and at his first chance took the

First Communion class. Then he started dragging his friends to church.

Later, when the church had started to take off, it was confronted with the bigotry and misunderstanding of the growing, changing population. With the sheriff leading the charge against the Latino immigrant community, the church banded together, choosing to fight for its survival. Not always successful, it lost three members to deportation and three families to lack of work. One woman is still struggling with Immigration and Customs Enforcement. Her son was arrested and was to be transferred to Texas. She won his release on her cognizance but was arrested for immigration violations when she went to pick him up. On behalf of her three U.S.-citizen children, she pled for a waiver. After a letter from Pastor Eickmann attesting to her character, her request was granted, only to be appealed. She still waits for the decision.

Through the obstacles facing the congregation, the church has struggled and worked and fought to create what each congregation strives for: true community and true family, a manifestation of Christ coming to all nations.

River of Life Lutheran Church—ELCA

Minneapolis, Minnesota
Interviewee—Pam Bloom

In 2000, Zion Lutheran Church, located in a neighborhood scarred with poverty and violence in Minneapolis, was concerned with its survival. The community was changing, attendance was dwindling, and the congregation was aging. The congregation prayed, believing that God would send people from the immediate neighborhood to be a part of Zion's ministry. They were pleasantly surprised when the congregation was infused with life from the Liberian and West African community who commuted from the suburbs to this inner city congregation. The newcomers became members of Zion and were active participants in a consolidation with Bethlehem Lutheran Church that resulted in River of Life Lutheran Church, a congregation where approximately a third of the members are from the immigrant community.

The Liberians embraced full participation in the congregation, braving blizzards and sharing their stories. During the adult Sunday School class, they shared stories of faith during the most horrific of times, stories of friends and family killed, wives and daughters sexually assaulted while family members were forced to watch, nursing babies torn from the arms of their mothers and thrown into the ocean, a massacre during Sunday worship at a Lutheran church.

By opening themselves to their new church family, each community was blessed as congregants' hearts were truly opened. Longtime members identified with their new brothers and sisters, recognizing and appreciating these wonderful, strong people. Today church potlucks are a wonderful mixture of lefse, lutefisk, African soup and fufu. Liberians read scripture during worship, sing in a praise group and in the traditional choir. They visit the sick, provide transportation, offer hospitality, and serve on the church council. As they graciously give congregants beautiful African gowns, not only are they us but we are also them.

Salem Lutheran Church—ELCA

Catonsville, Maryland
Interviewee—Irene Amoros

Welcoming refugees through cosponsorship has been a part of Salem Lutheran Church's history for three decades. Through the years, church members have raised money, gathered household goods and clothing, and provided transportation, housing, jobs, and friendship to several families of refugees from various countries.

In 2004, Salem welcomed another family to a new life in the United States through cosponsorship. Originally from Sudan, this family was living in a refugee camp in Cairo, Egypt, for five years before they came to America. The couple's two youngest children were born in the refugee camp.

They had been married in a civil-service ceremony in the refugee camp. Deeply religious, it disturbed this young couple that their marriage ceremony was not performed and blessed in a church. They would not allow themselves to receive communion at Salem because of this. When Pastor G. Edward Whetstone informed Salem members of this sad fact, the congregation's welcoming response was to throw a wedding for this couple! After reciting their vows to one another in front of God and a packed congregation, their marriage covenant was blessed by Pastor Whetstone. He then blessed the elements for communion and the couple came to the altar rail, knelt down, and received communion for the first time as a married couple. They have continued to participate in the life of the congregation as members and their children (now numbering five) attend Sunday School regularly.

St. Peter's Lutheran Church—LCMS

Brooklyn, New York

Away from the frantic bustle of Times Square, far from the glamorous rush of Manhattan, the Bangladeshi community of New York City has established itself within the diversity of Brooklyn. Cloistered by language, the community often lacks connection to its English-speaking neighbors. St. Peter's Lutheran Church of Brooklyn has reached out to the immigrant population, spreading its ministry.

The congregation reflects the community as the members and their ministries also touch the Hispanic, Caribbean, and Korean populations around them. The church has been intentional in its position, preferring to be among this multiplicity of cultures rather than the sameness of the suburbs. Encountering the changes in the neighborhood, the church has expanded its ministries, moving to serve those most in need.

Recently that need has come from the growing Bangladeshi population. Isolated and without English training, they find themselves separated from the flow of New York life. The Rev. James Roy of St. Peter's speaks Bengali and has started English classes to reach out to these recent, secluded immigrants, offering a hand of friendship. Integral to the classes, students receive a personal tutor who acts as an English-speaking friend, inviting the newcomers to meals with the church. Although many of the pupils are Muslim, they welcome the connection. Building broader relationships, both communities are enriched by the exchanges of culture and knowledge.

Trinity Evangelical Lutheran Church—LCMS

Cleveland, Ohio
Interviewee—Pastor Jeff Johnson

Emily Dickinson wrote about hope as a thing with feathers, ceaselessly singing the tune without the words as it perches on the soul. As Christians, the congregation of Trinity Evangelical Lutheran Church in Cleveland, Ohio, finds that hope in faith. Through faith, they follow the melody, even as it leads them beyond the familiar words.

As an expression of faith, they founded Building Hope in the City. Building Hope in the City is a collection of ministries to plant churches, renew the missions of existing churches, and send God's people into service. In so doing, it touches immigrant and refugee communities that have been marginalized by policy and poverty. Rising out of the renewed ministry at Trinity, Building Hope began with a vision of Lutheran revitalization and church planting, but it has become a story of individuals.

Before embarking on a mission of community revitalization, the congregation was confronted with the truth of James 2:26: "Faith without works is dead." Trinity Evangelical Lutheran Church had become a cultural relic. After 140 years of worship in Cleveland, the congregation had gone static. When Pastor Jeff Johnson came to Trinity in 1992, he had the task of reviving the spirit of the church. Under his leadership, the congregation seized upon James's words and threw themselves into service. They looked around at their neighbors and embraced their differences. Now, membership reflects that work. The 281 congregants mirror the communities touched by Trinity's service, drawing new Latino, African, and Arabic immigrants to mix with the European immigrants of generations past. Ministries to meet the needs of the African and Arab communities have begun, reaching out to them in different ways. A Lebanese couple was recruited to touch the Palestinian and Egyptian populations. They began leading worship services in December 2008. Trinity heard the call to minister to those that society neglects. In Cleveland, this means embracing immigrant communities and welcoming all as brothers and sisters in Christ.

{ 8 }

What Next?

Churches don't just happen. They grow out of love and faith and commitment—which is to say that they grow out of a passion for Christ, the gospel, and the people God loves. First love is always the most passionate, always more willing to take on risk for the sake of the beloved. If we are going to become a church that passionately welcomes the stranger in the name of Christ, we have to recover the first love that brought the church into existence two thousand years ago and that brought our own congregations into existence over the last few hundred years.

First Love

On Sunday, November 1, 1903, a small group of the faithful, passionate about mission, gathered together in the storeroom of a grocery store owned by Ernst C. Schumacher in Bay Ridge, Brooklyn. John Holthusen, pastor of Trinity Lutheran Church, was called to open a mission and begin organizing a congregation to serve the German immigrant community. In September

1904, the Brooklyn Mission Society called the Rev. Paul G. Lindemann as missionary to Bay Ridge. The congregation just celebrated the one hundred and fifth anniversary of a strong ministry with a senior center and an elementary school serving all ages in the neighborhood.

At Good Shepherd, Pearl River, New York, hangs a picture of a confident group of dreamers, hats in hand, whose first love pushed them to organize the congregation by canvassing the neighborhoods and raising funds for a church.

Ella Luttmann, an elderly resident of Queens, remembers going door to door as a child in Long Island City, Queens, inviting her friends and neighbors to the first English language Sunday School at Trinity. Before she moved to Queens she had been a member of a Manhattan German congregation. Because she dallied at the candy store, she was late for a Sunday School picnic on the harbor cruise boat *Slocum* and did not get on the doomed craft. Until September 11, 2001, that was the greatest disaster in New York's history—hundreds of German immigrant Sunday School children drowned in the East River. Ninety years later, still experiencing first love, she was one of those who welcomed the first Korean language Lutheran ministry in the United States to Atonement Lutheran in Jackson Heights, Queens.

These stories recall that first mission passion, that first love, that drove the ministry of those new congregations.

Ephesus: Anatomy of a New Church

The church in Ephesus serves as a model of the life cycle of a congregation or a synod and as a model of the journey of a disciple of Jesus. The church in Ephesus is mentioned in four different places in the New Testament. It provides a portrait of church planting that has been repeated in the birthing of every one of our congregations and every new ministry.

Passionate Planting and Great Commission Love—
Acts 19, 20

Paul and his cohorts were sent by the Council of Jerusalem. Today, missionaries and support sent by others give birth to the faith communities that give profound meaning to our lives today. One can trace the marks of mission in the birth of the Ephesian church:

- the exercise of charismatic gifts, miraculous expectation
- the overthrowing of demons, a healing presence;
- an organized ministry;
- a public message and controversy over it;
- the establishment of a missionary center;
- the making of disciples.

Some of you reading this book are leaders of young congregations organized within the past few years. Think of the new mission starts in your synod or your conference. Think of the other ministries started by thriving congregations with mission in mind. Think of the hundreds of new immigrant congregations or worshipping communities started by the ELCA and LCMS in the past year. Like the church in Ephesus, these new missions are a part of a church body that sees itself as a minority on a mission with a message about Jesus our Lord.

A Church's Life and Message Matures—Paul's Letter to the Ephesians

In his letter to the Ephesians, Paul addresses a maturing church, giving them ethical, theological, and churchly guidance. Paul did not have manuals or training in mission, so he had to teach by example, writing letters, and equipping other leaders. His passionate planting of this church is taking root: disciples are

emerging in the Ephesian mission. The community of faith in
Ephesus is marked by:

- shared doctrine: the teaching of forgiveness, of salvation
  by grace, of oneness in Christ;
- life together: the experience of unity, of diverse gifts, of
  holy living, of common ethics, and a common identity
  in Christ;
- continuity: strong relationships with Paul and the other
  churches, and pastoral continuity in the ministries of
  Tychichus and Timothy.

Many of you reading this book are leaders of congregations that are maturing in their ministry, building and expanding. Some of your congregations have celebrated anniversaries
of twenty-five years or more. Others are much older. Some of
you who are reading this book are leaders of congregations
in the midst of building campaigns or are contemplating one.
Like the church depicted in the book of Ephesus, the message
of the gospel has taken hold among you and the life of your
congregation is deepening and maturing and growing.

Church Order and Leadership Organization—Paul to Timothy

Maturing churches organize for growth. They seek committed
pastoral ministries to strengthen their roots, to keep them on
track. Paul taught such leadership: "I urge you [Timothy] to
remain in Ephesus so that you may instruct certain people not
to teach any different doctrine . . . The aim of such instruction
is love that comes from a pure heart, a good conscience, and
sincere faith" (1 Timothy 1:3).

Over time the message and communal life of the church in Ephesus matures, and the gift of leadership is given to the church. At every ordination, every installation of a bishop, every commissioning of an associate in ministry, and every diaconal "setting apart," we read instructions from Paul's letters to Timothy. Some of you reading this book are rostered leaders in the church. These words of Paul to Timothy and the leaders of the Ephesian church have been spoken to you: "I remind you to rekindle the gift of God that is within you through the laying on of hands; for God did not give us a spirit of cowardice, but rather a spirit of power and of love and of self-discipline" (2 Timothy 1:6-7). Paul envisions in his letter to Timothy a church in Ephesus—and churches in every time— marked by bishops, pastors, deacons, elders, and all Christians living examples of faith in daily life.

In Acts, Ephesians, and Paul's letters to Timothy, we can trace the outline of a church planted in passionate risk taking and believers filled with ardent love for the gospel. We are descended from Ephesus. We have a church with the same message, protocols for leadership, and a distinctive way of life in the world. What is missing?

A Church Empty at the Heart—The Book of Revelation

In his letter to the church in Ephesus, the writer of Revelation notes their growing and maturing message. They have endured persecution, opposed false doctrine, and have not grown weary in their life together. But he has one charge against them. They have lost their first love and the mission excitement that drives the passionate planting of the gospel in their midst (Revelation 2:1-7).

Recovering Our First Love in the ELCA: A Church Again in Mission

We believe that the ELCA, in the passion of its first love, will be a church that embraces the stranger, welcomes all people, and has a vital mission in the increasingly global American community. To embrace the immigrant among us is to recapture and embrace both the Great Commission and the Great Commandment. The world is coming to our shores, our neighborhoods, our congregations. Indeed, it is already here. The invitation to stand with the immigrant is a call to be engaged in the continual reformation of a church in mission. It is also an invitation to receive the many gifts that the stranger in our midst brings to us.

Historian and theologian Jaraslov Pelikan once said that Lutherans have never had the opportunity to be catholic (universal), only ethnic. Our opportunity to be catholic has arrived. When Salem Danish Lutheran in Brooklyn becomes Salaam Arabic Lutheran, Lutheran catholic identity and mission has arrived. In many ways the development of the ELCA and of our synods and congregations mirrors the Ephesian experience. With high hopes twenty-five years ago, we came together from our predecessor communions: AELC, ALC, and LCA. For twenty-five years we have planted many new missions and celebrated communal defeats and victories. Our ministries of mission and service have matured through the World Hunger Fund, the Companion Synod program, Lutheran Disaster Response, Lutheran Service in America, and other services.

The culture of our church organization is being transformed as we renew missional structures to create a more grassroots church. Leadership development has resulted in greater diversity among pastors, deacons, and lay leaders. If we listen carefully, we can hear the words of Revelation to the church at Ephesus being spoken to us as well: "You have abandoned the love you had at first. . . . Repent and do the works you did at first" (Revelation 1:4-5). First love is renewed when we allow ourselves to be stunned again by the resurrection of Jesus from the dead.

Stunned by the Resurrection of Jesus

Saul never got over his encounter with the risen Christ on the road to Damascus. Stunned by the resurrection of Jesus from the dead, his life was changed forever. Jesus' resurrection was the catalytic power of God's ecstatic mission. The first love is God's, for God so loved the world that he sent Jesus. The death and resurrection of Jesus is behind the passion of every new ministry, every rescued soul.

This book began at Ground Zero in New York, and the many feet on the road for rescue and recovery. Jerusalem is another Ground Zero. The paschal mystery of the death and resurrection of Jesus is, for Christians, the Ground Zero of our narrative of faith. We became friends on the road, amigos en pie, when Jesus rose from the dead.

Easter caused a track meet. It seems that when Jesus rose from the dead it got a lot of people on their feet. Those running to the tomb on Easter, those walking back and forth, were all amigos en pie. When word got out that Jesus was missing, that the tomb was empty, there was a lot of running around. Mary Magdalene, early in the morning, got on her feet and went to the tomb. She saw the stone rolled away but did not go in. The tomb was empty. She thought all was lost. The tomb represented defeat, grief, hopelessness, despair. She ran and told

Peter, "They have taken the Lord out of the tomb, and we do not know where they have laid him."

Hearing the news of the empty tomb, Peter and John got on their feet. Peter walked in and saw the wrappings. Then the beloved one went in, and Scripture says, "He believed." Mary, still on her feet, returned to the tomb. She was weeping. Two angels appeared, but she did not know who they were. She did not recognize Jesus when he stood before her; she thought he was dead. She thought he was the gardener; she thought he had taken her Lord away. Then she heard him speak her name. When he spoke her name she suddenly knew who he was—her beloved teacher, Jesus—and she also knew who she was—his beloved. She had a new identity in the risen Christ; we all do.

The Gospel of Matthew promises that when we welcome the stranger we encounter the risen Lord. In that encounter, like Mary, we come to know more deeply who we are—both individually and as a community of faith. Jesus' promise to Peter is a promise to us as well: "I will give you other brothers, sisters, mothers, fathers." When we welcome the stranger, the family of God expands, and we discover that we all belong to each other in the power and promise of the resurrected Christ. The encounter with the risen Christ in our encounter with "the least of these" is the driving force behind Christian hospitality to and service on behalf of immigrants. Everything we do on behalf of our new neighbors flows from the power and promise of the resurrection and our new being in Christ.

Our first love is the God who loved us, came to us, saved us, and calls us in Jesus the Christ. Our second love is the world God loves. Following the resurrection, Jesus gathered his followers and sent them out as amigos en pie, friends on the road, with these words of call and promise: "All authority in heaven and on earth has been given to me. Go therefore and make disciples of all nations, baptizing them in the name of the Father and of the Son and of the Holy Spirit, and teaching them to obey everything that I have commanded you. And remember, I am with you always, to the end of the age. (Matthew 28:18-20). Christ's command—the command of the One who loved us to and beyond death—is all the motivation we need to get up on our feet and go to meet the strangers among us.

Opening Locked Doors of Fear

After the crucifixion, the dispirited, despairing followers of Jesus hid themselves behind locked doors because they were afraid. Fear has created the paralyzing conditions of hostility and polarization in our country that surround immigrants and the issues they bring to our common life. In this climate of fear, we need to hear the call of our first love. The risen Lord enters our locked doors of fear and says, "Peace be with you. As the Father has sent me, so I send you" (John 20:19, 21).

The Fears We Feel

There is a sense of weariness and fear among us in both the ELCA and in the broader culture as we struggle with issues of human sexuality in which we have no consensus. It is too often a polarizing issue in which we forget that we are talking about real people, often fellow saints in baptism, always beloved children of God. Our communal love runs cold as the conflict over human sexuality puts us on the defensive, drives us to attack, or moves us to troubled silence.

Economic pressure adds to our fear and contributes to our mutual estrangement. In the church, pressures on national, synodical, and congregational budgets are being driven by rising health care costs, a weak economy, and other economic factors. In the wider culture, those same economic pressures drive us to see others who want a seat at the table of abundance as threats to our own wellbeing.

Pastors fear that with dwindling resources they will be abandoned by the church. Older congregations fear the loss of vitality and relevance as they continue to hold on while membership and resources dwindle. These fears are real and they cause great tension in the body of Christ. But when we recall together our first love we need not be afraid: "I am with you always, to the end of the age." When Christ, our first love, is with us, what shall we fear? (See Romans 8:31-19.)

We continue to try to find the courage to name our spiritual malaise. When the fires of our first love for God and second love for our neighbors have grown cold, what we have is a failure of pastoral and prophetic leadership. When our members continue to share only 1.7 percent of the blessings God has given them for the work of the church, and when they fail to put their feet on the road of service, we have a crisis of discipleship. When many congregations throughout the ELCA share nothing for the wider work of the church through their synod and church body, we have a relational crisis in our shared sense of church and mission. But we can face these spiritual crises without fear.

Reclaiming the Great Commission and the Great Commandment as the cornerstone of our life as a church in mission—including outreach to and solidarity with our immigrant neighbors—is not a program or a technique. It is a continual reorientation of our hearts, minds, souls, bodies, and resolve toward the resurrection of Jesus, toward the love of the Good Shepherd for the lost sheep. It calls forth ardent gratitude for the passionate birthing of our own congregations, for the new missions among us, for our immigrant ancestor stories, for our own baptismal faith.

We Are Lutheran and We Are Pro-Immigrant

We have shared many ways that individuals and congregations can engage immigrants and the issues and gifts they bring to our communal life. There must also be corporate responses by the whole church. We outline three of these: planting the church, public theological witness and advocacy, and an immigration task force in every synod.

Church Planting

When the Romans reached the shore of Old Britain, they dragged their boats ashore and burned them on the beach. The message was blunt and clear. We are here to stay. For twenty-five years the ELCA has been a church body where only three percent of its membership is non-white with a primary language other than English.

There have and continue to be strategies for multicultural engagement and growth. It seems there is an ethnic strategy on every desk in the national church. But that three percent number has been persistent and implacable. And it will not change until we Lutherans "burn our boats on the shore." Until national priorities and strategies become local, until we together plant and renew the church where the people live, we will have only the comfort of our convictions. Immigration is the meta issue for what America is becoming. To burn our boats on the new shore of this emerging multicultural America is to invest in congregations that are connected to their communities. We need new communities of word and sacrament and current congregations reconnecting to their communities. It is at the local font and altar—Schechem and Bethel—where strategies for multicultural growth are transformed into flesh and blood ministries of hospitality and care.

Many congregations, some of them lifted up in this book, are vibrant communities of Jesus making a difference in the lives of immigrant people. But a recent study by the Resource and Evaluation Unit of the ELCA has revealed that new mission congregations are not thriving and not growing from dependence to sustainable local ownership. Our new starts in immigrant communities and in communities of poverty are doing even worse and are even more vulnerable and dependent on outside support. Too many of these ministries are dying, closing, or barely hanging on.

We are out of relationship at the grassroots level where the church lives. Local congregations watch new ministries planted in their midst struggle and sometimes close. In the way of Jesus, no congregation ought to struggle and die alone. We are not connected to one another in real, missional struggle. Too often our congregations have lost their connection to their communities and the everyday struggles and issues of their neighbors, including immigrants. Mission initiative needs to return to the grassroots of the church. The ELCA is renewing its way of starting and renewing congregations. All mission is local.

What would it look like for every synod of the ELCA to have a bishop with the resolve and accountability for planting the church in the midst of our new neighbors? What would it look like for every conference, cluster, or local ministerium to be a platform for evolving mission strategies? What would it look like for new mission starts to have local partners and support right at the time of birth?

What if these local conference strategies were formed by collective faith practices? When engaging the local community in mission, communal spiritual practices such as worship, prayer, the study of Scripture, discernment, stewardship, and advocacy take on an urgency and spiritual depth that renews both church and community.

The ELCA is calling and sending a Director for Evangelical Mission to each synod to sit at the table and work with the staff of the local missionary bishop in order that the resources and institutional strength of the larger church can accompany these local efforts. We are organizing an apostolate to and with our new immigrant neighbors. It is not enough for the national church to pass statements, advocate, and provide material assistance on behalf of immigrants. When "they" really become "us" there will be a new integrity in all areas of the church's life, but especially in a growing cadre of congregations engaging their immigrant neighbors in their life and mission.

This is happening already around the country. In Toledo, Kansas City, Milwaukee, Western North Dakota, New Orleans, and in urban, suburban, and rural settings, congregations are coming together to dwell in the Word, renew their relationships, embrace their communities, plant new congregations, and renew old congregations for the sake of the gospel. Church-based community organizing has been an ally. In Florida, every conference sent a mission strategy team to a gathering of missional leaders with the clear conviction that a conference is now a platform for mission planning and execution. When we are in renewed relationships across the church, we can then imagine an apostolate to our new neighbors. One hundred new starts and renewed ministries among our immigrant neighbors every year is realistic.

Re-Rooting in the Community: One Example of Local Church Planting

The Northeast Queens Conference engaged in a synodical Re-Rooting in the Community process. Most of its congregations were struggling; some were very near closing. The neighborhoods of the conference were filled with new immigrants. Flushing, New York, has the largest Korean community in the United States. This process is similar to many in use throughout the ELCA and its ecumenical partners. The congregations, schools, social ministry organizations, and other Lutheran and ecumenical institutions join together in a discipline of prayer and discernment, study of Scripture, listening, training, and relationship building as they do strategic planning for mission.

These building blocks of the process are central to any approach that is effective and faithful:

- The process is shaped by the presence of Jesus in word and sacraments. The initial training sessions lift up the centrality of word and sacraments and present stories from the biblical drama that illuminate listening, mentoring, building community, leadership development, and public mission. The participants in these sessions covenant to join together in the process.
- Training in conducting one-on-one interviews and small group "house meetings" leads to a disciplined listening presence in both the parish and the community. This listening presence is the heartbeat of the process, as living testimony is shared by member and neighbor, grassroots ownership of proposals is developed, real issues are identified and addressed, and the church is exposed to potential new leaders.

- Strategic "dream teams" for the conference and each institution lift up issues and implications for mission by analyzing the interviews and collected demographic and statistical data.
- Several conference consultations wrestle with these issues and implications as mutual support and solidarity in mission emerges.
- The conference and each institution draft a mission statement.
- Concrete proposals for the mission of the conference and each institution are developed.
- Throughout the process, training sessions are held in evangelism, leadership development, word and sacrament-centered mission. Worship, prayer, and Bible study keep the process centered on Christ.

In a process such as this the future of our institutions is secured by turning their lives toward the larger community, its human need, and those without the church in their lives. The process becomes a platform where tough institutional decisions can be made about the future viability of individual congregations in renewed relationships. And collective action can be brought to emerging mission opportunities. This was the experience of the Northeast Queens process. The listening in the community gave human testimony to demographic evidence of a burgeoning South Asian community that would respond to outreach. The local mission team of the conference set the table for this ministry.

To the table came national partners from the Division for Outreach, Multicultural Ministries, the pastor of the first ELCA South Asian mission in Chicago, and synodical leaders. Durable, sustaining partnerships were formed for funding, launching, and sustaining the mission. St. Paul Lutheran

Church in Floral Park, Queens, was chosen as the best site. It was struggling for survival, had a great facility, and its leadership was ready because, in the re-rooting process, they had renewed their relationships to the other conference congregations and the synod leadership. A local conference mission team coordinated the process.

A pastor from the Andra Pradesh Lutheran church in India, which was doing a similar outreach to South Asians in Hong Kong, accepted the call to begin the South Asian ministry in Queens. The local mission team and the synod Mission Director welcomed the new pastor and his family, built an apartment in St. Paul's large facility, and walked with them as the ministry began. The ministry was named "Ashirwad" (divine blessing in Sanskrit). Its mission and programs matured into a growing congregation in close relationship with the English speaking members of St. Paul's. The neighborhood outreach, with ecumenical and interfaith support, became a critical outreach into the immigrant community beyond South Asians. The conference congregations joined to form a conference youth ministry. Finally, the growing congregation, while not losing its South Asian focus, organized as St. Paul International Lutheran Church, and it today serves people from around the world.

We understand how the church accompanied our immigrant forbears as they built their families and made a stand in the new world. Brooklyn is known as the "borough of churches," and along the Gowanus Expressway the sky is pierced by steeples rising from the working class streets, a testimony to immigrant builders' hopes and dreams and faith. Driving over the bridges of the city and along the Long Island Expressway in Queens, the domes of mosques join the spires and steeples, marking the immigrant soul. They wanted touches of beauty and faith in this new land. Their world was grey and drab, and they wanted more. In these houses of worship, immigrants of years long past and today have been able to pray, "O prosper the work of our hands!" (Psalm 90:17).

As the church renews its congregations by helping them reconnect to their communities, they become sacred spaces where our new neighbors can pray that God would prosper the work of their hands—work they are willing to do—for them and for their children.

Word and Sacrament as Mission

Benedictine liturgical scholar Aidan Kavanaugh has said that the integrity of evangelism is directly related to the integrity of the liturgy. Mission is the legs we put on our prayers and liturgical practice. Embedded in the move toward local congregations in relationship with their conference and synod is the conviction that baptism and eucharist have inherent missional power.

We do not baptize new Christians and leave them at the font. It is baptismal ministry to follow them into the world. To care and struggle for the schools in which they learn, the communal values that shape them, the nature of their relationships, whether they have mentors. A vision of a well-lived life in society is baptismal mission. In the eucharist, we not only eat at the altar table of our congregations, but we follow the real presence of Jesus into the world to connect with the community. Baptism and eucharist are public. Eating, drinking, claiming, and nurturing help us maintain an intense focus on local community, help us care for the life of the world.

Immigration Task Force in Every Synod

Several years ago, synod assemblies passed a resolution that went to the Churchwide Assembly where it also passed. The resolution called on each synod to form an immigration task force. Such task forces have yet to be organized in all synods.

The Metropolitan New York Synod's Immigration Task Force went public in June of 2006, when over two hundred people attended a town hall meeting at Trinity in Sunset Park, Brooklyn, in support of immigration ministries in the synod. The tone of the meeting, and the Immigration Task Force, was set by Chung Wha Hong, the director of the New York Immigration Coalition. She reminded us that "every twenty years or so America is called to remember its values. Movements develop to reclaim the guiding principles of what it means to be an American. Today the situation surrounding immigration reform and the migrant is what the civil rights and the anti-war movement were during the 1950s and 60s."

The success of that meeting was that the Immigration Task Force deliberately tried to enter into the breach between the faith community, social activists, and service providers. Lutheran speakers and leaders at the meeting were immigrant pastors and lay leaders. The meeting was translated into Spanish, Arabic, Mandarin, Cantonese, and Russian. Ecumenical and local immigration leaders spoke on a variety of topics. Others spoke on health care for immigrants, fundamentals of immigration law, housing and immigrants, and other issues.

The synod immigration task forces should be formed in relationship to the local conference and synodical mission tables. Synod immigration task forces should be central to the mission planning that will plant new and renewed mission congregations among our immigrant neighbors. Mission cannot be divorced from advocacy, social change, and social service. It is all part of Christ's mission in the world.

Public Theology: A Missional Church Accompanying Civil Society

Finally, public witness to immigration issues and all issues of poverty, hunger, and justice have integrity when such witness is linked to local congregations. The grassroots will inform the global, and public theology and advocacy will inform the local. Local public theology supports the local church in reaching out to and with our immigrant neighbors.

Lutheran Immigration and Refugee Service has the best reputation for refugee resettlement in the country. It is a unique combination of congregations and professionals in the field. When Haitian and Central American asylum seekers began to arrive (and the term "illegal aliens" was coined), LIRS got out in front of the issue, raising and delivering significant financial support to local groups, building a network for "detention watch," and helping develop a public theology around these issues. LIRS programs are cutting-edge and place Lutherans in the forefront of the nation on immigration issues. When you combine local and national Lutheran efforts with the efforts of the international Lutheran community through Lutheran World Relief and the Lutheran World Federation, you have the potential to make a real difference in the lives of those caught in the breach.

The global debate about migration is begging for insight, faith, and bold ideas. In the past ten years, one third of immigrants to the U.S. have been undocumented. We need conversation about how to make migration a positive experience for both migrants and the sending and receiving nations. We need migration that is safe, positive, legal, regulated, and humane. It is a conversation that brings together business and labor, the Latino, Asian, African, Eastern European communities, and other immigrant and migrant communities. The issues surrounding Latino immigration are particularly pressing in that Latinos are the largest and fastest growing "minority" in our country.

We believe that the ELCA should be a leader in the conversation. A Lutheran public theology, in dialog with our many ecumenical and interfaith partners, could be the catalyst for new, positive approaches to immigration policy and reform. We are in a position to gather the many "dangling conversations" into one new conversation, pushing new questions but always bringing to the table those "on the ground"—documented and undocumented immigrants and migrants and those who serve them.

We need to feel with the heart, think with the head, and help with the hand. So far the level of thinking on these issues has not been up to the opportunities and challenges before us. The tension between security concerns and immigration policy has only hardened. The conversation we need is both local and global, both ecumenical and interfaith, about both policy and practice. It is the "big conversation" of this new century, and Lutherans have a theology, constituency, institutions, and relationships around the word and around the block that we bring to the conversation as both leaven and light.

This is a public conversation worthy of engagement at every area of the church's life. It will involve the seminaries, colleges, and universities of the ELCA, as well as centers for public theology across the ecumenical and interfaith landscape. It may call for a "seminary of the streets" that identifies immigrant leaders from local communities and accompanies them in planting immigrant ministries and congregations. It will need congregations to study books like this one—especially the biblical texts embedded in the argument of this book and others. It will involve planting new ministries. In all of it, we will discover once again that in the way of Jesus, and in the power of the resurrection, *they are us.*

Walking Together into God's Future

We close with a vision of the future that we believe that God is calling us to build together. Here is Stephen's account of Good Friday, 2007, at Trinity Lutheran Church, Long Island City, Queens, New York.

Trinity's sanctuary darkened progressively as candles were extinguished during the reading of the Passion according to St. John. At the conclusion of the starkly beautiful Tenebrae service, I walked in silence with the congregation to the rear of the darkened church and opened the narthex doors to pilgrims walking down 37th Street. An endless line of candles illuminated the darkness as parishioners of Most Precious Blood parish approached the church. These were pilgrims walking the Via Dolorosa, the Way of the Cross. On this night, Trinity was the Fourth Station of the Cross: "Jesus meets his afflicted mother."

On and on they came, a flowing band of more than a thousand amigos en pie, "friends on foot," carrying banners, processional crosses, and garlanded floats of Mary and of a recumbent Jesus under a coffin of glass, and holding aloft a huge crucifix with agonized body. Above the sounds of feet striking concrete, I heard the amplified chanting of Kyrie Eleison, "Lord have mercy," led by the parish priest. The haunting sound of those many footsteps reverberates still in my memory.

Thousands of feet formed a human chain of immigrants, praying in Polish, Croatian, Italian, Spanish, Arabic, Mandarin, and German as they walked, bearing the cross of Jesus through the streets of Queens. I glimpsed America's future in those feet from many places, in the life-long neighborhood faithful and their new immigrant neighbors walking together in faith—partners in the re-enchantment of the city.

The crowd turned onto 31st Avenue and waited as the huge statue of the Blessed Virgin Mary, borne by fifteen strong men, followed the ministers into Trinity's sanctuary. (I imagined I could hear our Nordic Lutheran forebears turn over in their graves as she entered.) In that moment I sensed the life of the neighborhood walking in too, along with the issues, the traditions, the needs, and the faith of those who now called this place home.

The men carried the Blessed Virgin back through the narthex and onto 31st Avenue, where the crowd stretched all the way to Steinway Street. "Were you there, when he saw his mother's face..." they sang. Archbishop Rene Valero, a fellow pastor who would become the first Spanish-speaking bishop in the Diocese of Brooklyn, handed me a microphone and I began a brief message, followed by the prayers for the Fourth Station of the Cross. Then the Lutherans from Trinity put their shoe leather on the ground and joined their Catholic brothers and sisters. We walked together following the cross through the streets of Queens, bearing witness to the faith that moves our feet, praying for the life of the world for which Christ died. Kyrie Eleison.

Questions for Reflection and Discussion

Introduction

1. Recall the last conversation you had or overheard about immigration.
   a. What was the overall tone?
   b. How would you describe the language or labels used about migrants?
   c. What was your emotional response?
   d. What questions did the conversation raise in your mind?
2. Frequently all foreign-born people who live in the U.S. are lumped into one category even though their situations are often worlds apart. Can you name at least three different categories of immigrants?
3. When you read scriptural and other faith-based admonitions to welcome the stranger, how do you apply them to immigration in the U.S. today? Or in what ways do you find it difficult to make such applications? Why?

Chapter 1

1. What is your September 11 story? How did that day change the way you see people, particularly immigrants?
2. Compare economic migrants in Scripture with economic migrants today. What is the same? What is different?
3. Trace the footsteps of your ancestors. What migration stories are part of your family identity?
4. Who are the 'wandering Arameans' in your life? In your community? What is being done to include them at the table?
5. What in particular about current immigration issues gets you up on your feet? What gets your congregation up on its feet?

Chapter 2

1. Reflect on the founders of your current congregation.
   a. Where did they come from? What push or pull factors motivated their migration? (This migration could be within the U.S. as well as to the U.S.)
   b. What did they hope to establish with this particular family of faith?
   c. What signs of their migration story and hopes remain (names, architecture, values, an so on)?
2. Name at least one major cultural change in the life of the congregation or its neighborhood since its founding. How has this change made the congregation stronger or how has it been a challenge to the congregation?
3. Are any of your current members or attendees immigrants of any kind? If so, what gifts and strengths have they brought to the life of the congregation? If not, how can your congregation begin to understand immigrant issues and invite immigrants into the community of faith?

Chapter 3

1. What about this chapter's history of immigration surprised you? Made you proud? Made you sad? Made you want to take action?
2. What did you notice about the pattern of exclusion over the decades?
3. How do you understand today's immigration policy? Do you think it is working or not working? Explain.
4. As U.S. citizens who are Christians, what do we do when it becomes apparent a law is not working well?

Chapter 4

1. Name at least three things that happen when Immigration and Customs Enforcement (ICE) raids a workplace.
   a. What positive changes can such a raid bring?
   b. What negative changes can such a raid bring?
2. Think back to the migration stories in your own family. How would they be different today?
3. What is the difference between a U.S. citizen and an undocumented migrant when it comes to deserving welcome and human care?

Chapter 5

1. Consider the shadows of your own community.
   a. Who is living in fear, living without dignity? Where are people being exploited? For whom is nothing prepared?
   b. What is scary about finding out?
2. Name one thing your congregation already does well and one abundant blessing already existing among members of

your community. With whom might they be shared in a sustainable way?

3. In what ways might you personally share a portion of your abundance or help to provide a path for vulnerable migrants?

Chapter 6

1. What story from your own congregation would you add to this chapter?

2. Which story might you use to motivate others in your congregation to open their hearts?

3. Imagine yourself passing this book on to a busy friend. If they were to read only one chapter or passage, which would it be and why?

Chapter 7

1. In what ways does the resurrection serve as the cornerstone on which to build a Christian mission to immigrants?

2. The Great Commandment calls us to love both God who made us and our neighbors. How are this "first love" and "second love" practically expressed in your congregation?

3. In what ways might your congregation begin to cooperate at the conference and synodical level in joint ministry to immigrants?

4. In what ways has your understanding of immigration issues been changed and what can be done to solve them as a result of reading this book?

Notes

Introduction

1. W.B. Yeats, "The Second Coming," in *The Collected Poems of W.B. Yeats* (New York: Simon and Schuster, 1996), 187.

2. Testimony given at Metropolitan New York Synod's Committee on Immigration, Good Shepherd Lutheran Church, Brooklyn, NY, June 23, 2006.

3. Quoted in Christine Pohl, *Making Room: Recovering Hospitality as a Christian Tradition* (Grand Rapids: Eerdmans, 1999), 6.

4. Bishop Stephen P. Bouman: "A Statement on Human Immigration Reform," Battery Park, Manhattan, February 1, 2006.

Chapter 1

1. John Dominic Crossan, *Jesus: A Revolutionary Biography* (San Francisco: Harper, 1994), 69.

2. Henry French, *Book of Faith Lenten Journey: 40-Days with the Lord's Prayer* (Minneapolis: Augsburg, 2008), 73.

Chapter Two

1. Major sources for this chapter are the historical timelines on the website of the Evangelical Lutheran Church in America (www.elca.org/Who-We-Are/History/Our-History-in-Context.aspx); and E. Theodore Bachmann and Mercia Brenne Bachmann, *Lutheran Churches in the World* (Minneapolis: Augsburg, 1989), 566-610.

2. *Thrivent Magazine* (Minneapolis, Spring 2006), 7. The history that follows is from the website of the Evangelical Lutheran Church in America: www.elca.org/Who-We-Are/History/Our-History-in-Context.aspx.

3. Bachmann and Bachmann, 608.

144 | They Are Us

4. Bachmann and Bachmann, 577.

5. We suspect that there were similar ministries in other port cities, but as of this writing we have not yet learned of them.

6. Richard W. Solberg, *Open Doors: The Story of Lutherans Resettling Refugees* (St. Louis: Concordia, 1992), 69.

Chapter 3

1. Aristide R. Zolberg, *A Nation By Design: Immigration Policy in the Fashioning of America* (Cambridge: Harvard University Press, 2006), 54-55.

2. Richard W. Solberg, *Open Doors: The Story of Lutherans Resettling Refugees* (St. Louis: Concordia, 1992), 14.

3. This function had previously been handled at Castle Clinton at the tip of Manhattan. After New York, the second major nineteenth-century immigration port of entry was Baltimore.

4. Solberg, 13-14.

5. Solberg, 30-31.

Chapter 4

1. Doris Meissner et al., *Immigration and America's Future: A New Chapter. Report of the Independent Task Force on Immigration and America's Future* (Washington: Migration Policy Institute, 2006), 2.

2. Tamar Jacoby, "Immigration Nation," *Foreign Affairs*, November/December 2006, 50-65.

3. Bishop Steven L. Ullestad, comments made in May 2008.

Chapter 5

1. Evangelical Lutheran Church of America, "A Message on Immigration," 1998, www.elca.org/socialstatements/immigration.

2. The Lutheran Church—Missouri Synod, "Joint Statement Regarding Immigration Concerns."

3. Evangelical Lutheran Church of America, "A Message on Immigration."

4. The painful history and legacy of slavery is a contradiction to this tradition and is recognized as such.

Chapter 6

1. Joy Dryfoos, *Adolescence at Risk: Prevalence and Prevention* (New York: Oxford University Press, 1991).